Nearing the Ye

Edward Thomas Hunter-Blair

Nearing the Year 2000

The Pentland Press Ltd
EDINBURGH

© Edward T. Hunter Blair 1990

First published in 1990 by
The Pentland Press Ltd
Kippielaw, by Haddington
East Lothian, Scotland

Printed and bound in Scotland by
D. & J. Croal Ltd., Haddington.

ISBN 0 946270 93 7

Je ne voulais pas dire à qui je dédiais ce livre

Cha robh cinnt agam

Aber jetzt wolle ich es zu Gott widmen

Contents

Front cover: Loch Ken from Parton Estate.
Photo, Allan Wright.

1

Thoughts for to-day

What is the meaning of existence? That is supposed to be one of the central philosophical questions, and I do not think it has been completely answered — except possibly in a religious sense — as yet.

I have been considering possible answers to this question since I was a lad, and the most I can say is that I am getting some relevant ideas on the subject.

There was a time (I was nine years old) when those around me thought I was as good as dead. My throat was blocked by flesh poisoned by Streptococcal bacteria. I had a high temperature, could not move and lay inert.

When I recovered I had a memory that although I could not move physically my soul or spirit was moving along a tunnel whose walls were red. The feeling was rather pleasant, and I was satisfied that I was going somewhere that I had no objection to going towards.

Then the progress of my spirit ceased. If anything I moved backwards in the tunnel the way I had come. Eventually I opened my eyes, and my body was on the way to recovery from near death.

As I was recovering it seemed that my heart had become strained, and I had to lie on my back for months following several heart attacks. When I was at last pronounced fully fit after some two years in all I was I suppose physically and mentally an unusual boy.

In later life I served for some time in the British Army and a doctor's report which I saw described me as "sensitive".

This probably was not meant as a compliment, but now I am willing to take pride in what I consider to be my unusual amount of sensitivity towards all kinds of things.

One subject I consider I am sensitive towards is the flow of international affairs. Perhaps I might be allowed to quote from what I wrote in my previous book, published in 1984. At the risk of earning a deplorable fame and notoriety (I said) as a False Prophet, I consider that as we approach the "Millenium" of 2000 A.D. there is a possibility — even a strong possibility — of events starting which could be described as a Whirlpool leading to a high and all-transforming Waterfall.

As we read the Press and consider the turn of events in public affairs, there seems to be a considerable public apprehension that we have entered into what could well be the beginning of a Nuclear Arms Race.

I am not one of those, however, who believe that the solution to impending problems necessarily lies in the direction of "Ban the Bomb" and "Unilateral Nuclear Disarmament".

It appears significant to me that the Nuclear Disarmament movement is strongest in the leading English-speaking countries of Great Britain and the U.S.A., together with those countries of Western and Central Europe which could well suffer most in any nuclear conflict between East and West.

Why are Disarmament and anti-nuclear movements so strong in the leading English-speaking countries? I would say that it is because there is a largely unexpressed feeling that there is a natural superiority to be found among English-speaking people; that the non-English speaking peoples and their languages are in the last resort only of secondary importance. This is expressed in the admitted failure of the overwhelming majority of the British and the Americans to learn any foreign language either at school or in their private or professional lives.

I think we should consider whether this feeling of Anglo-American superiority has any foundation on military, economic or political grounds, and also whether it could possibly lead to a reaction among the peoples who are not English-speaking which could be disastrous for Britain and the U.S.A.

I read recently a statement in a newspaper article that Russian is "the second most important language in the world". The article continued to say that studying Russian is no longer

2

popular in British schools, and that many British teachers who had qualified themselves to teach Russian were no longer teaching it, but rather French with in a few cases Spanish or German.

My own experience of a visit to the Soviet Union was a journey by air from Prestwick organized by "The Scotsman" newspaper, a member of the Thomson Group of companies. In the plane also were about an equal number of Lancashire folk, Thomson Group newspaper readers in the Lancashire area.

Our destination was Moscow and we spent about a week staying in a handsome new hotel near the Kremlin, built I would say on the multi-storey lines pioneered in the cities of the U.S.A.

Our Russian hosts made us very welcome, going to great pains looking after us and doing their best to keep us all interested and entertained. It was noticeable I think that the Scots enjoyed themselves more than the Lancashire folk, being more adaptable and ready to accept for the time being aspects of Russian living which differed from their own. Hardly any apart from myself were linguists, nearly all being perplexed by such simple aspects of life in Russia as the Slavonic Alphabet.

In 1983 I went with a party of members of the Scottish Landowners' Federation to attend the French Game Fair at Chantilly, near Paris. One evening we dined in a restaurant before going on to a late night Parade and Firework Display. About seven of us decided we would rather go back to our hotel from the restaurant. It was difficult to discover where to go to find a taxi. I am holder of a Certificate After Examination (First Class) of the University of Paris and no-one else seemed able or willing to ask in French where the taxis were (at Chantilly Station, in fact), find our way on foot, and then give the driver instructions where to go.

The people from the Scottish Landowners' Federation and the Thomson Newspaper readers were on the whole from those with a better education and wider outlook than the average among the British population. The general mass of the British population, and likewise of the U.S. population, are much worse educated, less adaptable and more limited in their outlook. Certainly they feel happier and more at home in Australia or New Zealand, for example, than in any typical European or Asiatic country unless they are visiting the latter for reasons of sunshine and holiday only.

Now that we know, more or less, what the main English-speaking nations think of the non-English speaking nations, we might wonder what some of the non-English speaking nations think of the English-speaking nations.

Speaking from a British point of view, I would say that the most important non-English speaking peoples are probably the Russians and the French.

We all know, or think we know, quite a lot about the Russians. The Soviet Union is the leading Communist power in the world and is trying all the time to increase Communism, and also its own power and boundaries. It is opposed in particular by the United States, which sees itself as the leader of Capitalism and anti-Communism. Each of the two leading countries tries all the time to find allies and friends throughout the world and to thwart the opposing power's activities.

The Soviet Union does not seem to be opposed to the English-speaking peoples as such. In fact the Soviet Union is notable for the comparative freedom and semi-independence it gives to the non-Russian peoples within its borders. Studies of the world's many peoples and languages are being made all the time within the U.S.S.R. Foreign languages are taught and learnt to a very considerable extent in the U.S.S.R. In contrast to England and the United States, the peoples of the U.S.S.R. are friendly on the whole towards all peoples and their cultures and languages.

Now let us consider France. After English and possibly Russian and Chinese, French is probably the next most important language in the world. There is a tradition of many centuries of dislike and rivalry between the English and French peoples, which the period of friendship and alliance dating from before the First World War has by no means ended. The French language derives mainly from Latin but has been influenced by the Gaullish language spoken in Julius Caesar's time. French has been roughly described as "Latin spoken with a Celtic accent". It seems particularly foreign to the English.

French people have always found the English difficult to understand and something of a problem to them. The French tend to be logical and rather intellectual. The English in general are far from being logical and have the ability to persuade themselves to believe almost anything regardless of the evidence. From the French point of view this is called "English hypocrisy".

4

Of all the European peoples, the French are the least ready to accept English as an international or world language. They would like French to occupy the leading position that it once did.

From a political point of view, France is reluctant to accept Anglo-American leadership. France's retirement from the North Atlantic Treaty Organization, which occurred in 1966, was a very significant action.

France's relations with Russia, and later with the Soviet Union, have since the beginning of this century usually been friendly. They are friendly to this day, despite a traditional friendship between France and the U.S.A. and the fact that France is associated with the Western Powers who are opposed to Communist Eastern Europe. The election to power of Mr Mitterand and his Socialist Government in France has strengthened ties with the U.S.S.R. Traditional French skill at diplomacy enables France to maintain a middle-of-the-road position between the Western and Eastern blocs.

As is well-known, the European Community, despite its elaborate organization, suffers from a continual tussle of power between the various countries represented. France is in fact the leader, supported by West Germany, the second most important member. Britain, despite efforts to enlist Italy or other countries as an ally, tends to be isolated (despite occasional support from the Netherlands and Belgium).

It is very doubtful whether the NATO alliance enjoys the active support of the majority of the population of the European Community countries. If war broke out, and particularly if the West were reluctant to use nuclear weapons, the East might well sweep the NATO forces Westward into the English Channel. I am doubtful that the Communist Eastern bloc forces could be necessarily held at the English Channel, though it is possible that the East/West boundary could well remain for a time at the English Channel.

In my opinion European countries, especially the civilian population, would not give very strong support to the West in an East/West conflict. Nor could the West necessarily count on strong support and assistance from countries outside Europe. Many Third World countries might even join the Eastern bloc, or at any rate stand as spectators on the side lines to see what happened.

In fact there are signs, associated with the possible

break-up of the European Community or Common Market, that a deep moral and political gulf is already forming or has formed at the English Channel. On one side are the English-speaking peoples, conservatively inclined, suspicious of foreigners and unable to understand or agree with them, and dependent on nuclear weapons and American money for their defence. On the other side are the European and some Asiatic peoples, Socialist-inclined, non-English speaking and rather less suspicious of each other than in the centuries prior to the First and Second World Wars.

I spent Christmas 1985 at the Atholl Centre, Pitlochry, which has been built by the Baptist Church as a conference and holiday centre.

My Christmas in the Highlands (Pitlochry is situated by the River Tummel, a tributary of the Tay, North of Perth) was most enjoyable and interesting. There was an atmosphere of devotion, of friendship and service to others, which I am sure we all appreciated.

Among the amenities at the Atholl Centre was a well-stocked book-stall or book-shop of religious and other books. I bought for a modest price a new copy of a recent edition of a book by the late Professor Clive Staples Lewis called "Miracles".

C. S. Lewis, as he is usually called, was of course a well-known writer on religious and other subjects. Unlike so many works of collections of sermons, prayers or on other religious topics, which are rather inclined to be dry and lack wider appeal and popularity, Professor Lewis's works, which include a series of stories for children, achieved a widespread appeal among many types of reader. Possibly his best-remembered book is "The Screwtape Letters", which purports to be a series of letters written by an elderly devil to edify his junior in the trade, in the subtle art of temptation.

I found this book called "Miracles" to be so significant that I would like to quote from it fairly extensively. The edition of which I bought a copy is published in the Fount series of paperbacks by William Collins & Co. Ltd. of London and Glasgow. The first edition was published in 1947.

In his book C. S. Lewis describes a Miracle as "an interference with Nature by supernatural power", though he says this is not the only definition possible.

What C. S. Lewis calls Nature is the natural world to

6

which we are all accustomed. He goes on to consider arguments in favour of the Supernatural.

"To some people the great trouble about any argument for the Supernatural is simply the fact that argument should be needed at all. If so stupendous a thing exists, ought it not to be as obvious as the sun in the sky?"

The fact which is in one respect the most obvious and primary fact, says Lewis, may be precisely the one that is most easily forgotten — forgotten not because it is so near or abstruse but because it is so near and so obvious. And that is exactly how the Supernatural has been forgotten. The Naturalists have been engaged in thinking about Nature. They have not attended to the fact that they were *thinking*. The moment one attended to this it is obvious that one's own thinking cannot be merely a natural event, and that therefore something other than Nature exists. The Supernatural is not remote and abstruse: it is a matter of daily and hourly experience, as intimate as breathing. Denial of it depends on a certain absent-mindedness. But this absent-mindedness is in no way surprising. You do not need — indeed you do not wish — to be always thinking about windows when you are looking at gardens through windows, or always thinking about eyes when you are reading.

In the same way the proper procedure for all limited and particular inquiries is to ignore the fact of your own thinking, and concentrate on the object. It is only when you stand back from particular inquiries and try to form a complete philosophy that you must take it into account. For a complete philosophy you must get in *all* the facts. In it you turn away from specialised or truncated thought to total thought: and one of the facts total thought must think about is Thinking itself. There is thus a tendency in the study of Nature to make us forget the most obvious fact of all. And since the Sixteenth Century, when Science was born, the minds of men have been increasingly turned outward, to know Nature and to master her. They have been increasingly engaged on those specialised inquiries for which truncated thought is the correct method. It is therefore not in the least astonishing that they should have forgotten the evidence for the Supernatural. The deeply ingrained habit of truncated thought — what we call the "scientific" habit of mind — was indeed certain to lead to Naturalism, unless this tendency was continually corrected from some other source. But no other source was at hand, for during the same period men of science were coming to be metaphysically and theologically uneducated.

This brings me to the second consideration. The state of affairs in which ordinary people can discover the Supernatural only by abstruse reasoning is recent and, by historical standards, abnormal. All over the world, until quite modern times, the direct insight of the mystics and the reasonings of the philosophers percolated to the mass of the people by authority and tradition; they could be received by those who were no great reasoners themselves in the concrete form of myth and ritual and the whole pattern of life. In the conditions produced by a century or more of Naturalism, plain men are being forced to bear burdens which plain men were never expected to bear before. We must get the truth for ourselves or go without it. There may be two explanations for this. It might be that humanity, in rebelling against tradition and authority, have made a ghastly mistake; a mistake which will not be the less fatal because the corruptions of those in authority rendered it very excusable. On the other hand, it may be that the Power which rules our species is at this moment carrying out a daring experiment.

Could it be intended that the whole mass of the people should now move forward and occupy for themselves those heights which were once reserved only for the sages? Is the distinction between wise and simple to disappear because all are now expected to become wise? If so, our present blunderings would be but growing pains. But let us make no mistake about our necessities. If we are content to go back and become humble plain men obeying a tradition, well. If we are ready to climb and struggle on till we become sages ourselves, better still. But the man who will neither obey wisdom in others nor adventure for her himself is fatal. A society where the simple many obey the few seers can live: a society where all were seers could live even more fully. But a society where the mass is still simple and the seers are no longer attended to can achieve only superficiality, baseness, ugliness, and in the end extinction. On or back we must go; to stay here is death.

One other point that may have raised doubt or difficulty should here be dealt with. I have advanced reasons for believing that a supernatural element is present in every rational man. The presence of human rationality in the world is therefore a

Miracle by the definition previously given. On realising this the reader may excusably say, "Oh, if *that's* all he means by a Miracle . . ." and fling the book away. But I ask him to have patience. Human Reason and Morality have been mentioned not as instances of Miracle (at least not the kind of Miracle you wanted to hear about) but as proofs of the Supernatural: not in order to show that Nature ever is invaded but that there is a possible invader. Whether you choose to call the regular and familiar invasion by human Reason a Miracle or not is largely a matter of words. Its regularity — the fact that it regularly enters by the same door, human sexual intercourse — may incline you not to do so. It looks as if it were (so to speak) the very nature of Nature to suffer *this* invasion. But then we might later find that it was the very nature of Nature to suffer Miracles in general. Fortunately the course of our argument will allow us to leave this question of terminology on one side. We are going to be concerned with other invasions of Nature — with what everyone would call Miracles. Our question could, if you liked, be put in the form, "Does Supernature ever produce particular results in space and time *except* through the instrumentality of human brains acting on human nerves and muscles".

I have said "*particular* results" because, on our view, Nature as a whole is herself one huge result of the Supernatural: God created her. God pierces her wherever there is a human mind. God presumably maintains her in existence. The question is whether He ever does anything else to her. Does he, besides all this, ever introduce into her events of which it would not be true to say, "This is simply the working out of the general character which He gave to Nature as a whole in creating her"? Such events are what are popularly called Miracles: and it will be in this sense only that the word Miracle will be used for the rest of the book.

The next chapter in "Miracles" which I find necessary to consider is called "Christianity and 'Religion'." The Christians say that God has done miracles. The modern world, even when it believes in God, and even when it has seen the defencelessness of Nature, does not. It thinks God would not do that sort of thing. Have we any reason for supposing that the modern world is right? I agree that the sort of God conceived by the popular "religion" of our own times would almost certainly work no miracles. The question is whether that popular religion is at all likely to be true.

I call it "religion" advisedly. We who defend our Christianity find ourselves constantly opposed not by the irreligion of our hearers but by their real religion. Speak about beauty, truth and goodness, or about a God who is simply the indwelling principle of these three, speak about a great spiritual force pervading all things, a common mind of which were are all parts, a pool of generalised spirituality to which we can all flow, and you will command friendly interest. But the temperature drops as soon as you mention a God who has purposes and performs particular actions, who does one thing and not another, a concrete, choosing, commanding, prohibiting God with a determinate character. People become embarrassed or angry. Such a conception seems to them primitive and crude and even irreverent. The popular "religion" excludes miracles because it excludes the "living God" of Christianity and believes instead in a kind of God who obviously would not do miracles, or indeed anything else. This popular "religion" may roughly be called Pantheism, and we must now examine its credentials.

In the first place it is usually based on a quite fanciful picture of the history of religion. According to this picture, Man starts by inventing "spirits" to explain natural phenomena; and at first he imagines these spirits to be exactly like himself. As he gets more enlightened they become less manlike, less "anthropomorphic" as the scholars call it. Their anthropomorphic attributes drop off one by one — first the human shape, then the human passions, then personality, will, activity — in the end every concrete or positive attribute whatever. There is left in the end a pure abstraction — mind as such, spirituality as such. God, instead of being a particular entity with a real character of its own, becomes simply "the whole show" looked at in a particular way or the theoretical point at which all the lines of human aspiration would meet if produced to infinity. And since, on the modern view, the final stage of anything is the most refined and civilised stage, this "religion" is held to be a more profound, more spiritual, and more enlightened belief than Christianity.

Now this imagined history of religion is not true. Pantheism certainly is (as its advocates would say) congenial to the modern mind; but the fact that a shoe slips on easily does not prove that it is a new shoe — much less that it will keep your feet dry. Pantheism is congenial to our minds not because it is the final stage in a slow process of enlightenment, but because it is almost as old as we are. It is immemorial in India. The Greeks rose above it only at their peak, in the thought of Plato and Aristotle; their successors relapsed into the great Pantheistic system of the Stoics.

Probably no thinking person would, in so many words, deny that God is concrete and individual. But not all thinking people, and certainly not all who believe in "religion", keep this truth steadily before their minds. We must beware, as Professor Whitehead says, of paying God ill-judged "metaphysical" compliments. We say that God is "infinite". In the sense that His knowledge and power extend to some things but not all, this is true. But if by using the word "infinite" we encourage ourselves to think of Him as a formless "everything" about whom nothing in particular and everything in general is true, then it would be better to drop that word altogether. Let us dare to say that God is a particular Thing. Once He was the only Thing: but He is creative, He made other things to be. He is not those other things. He is not "universal being": if He were there would be no creatures, for a generality can make nothing. He is "absolute being" — or rather *the* Absolute Being — in the sense that He alone exists in His own right.

C. S. Lewis speaks about our "repugnance to disorder". The disorderly world which we cannot endure to believe is the disorderly world He would not have endured to create. Our greatest natural philosopher thinks this also the metaphysic out of which the sciences originally grew. Professor Whitehead points out in 'Science and the Modern World' that centuries of belief in a God who combined the personal energy of Jehovah with the rationality of a Greek philosopher first produced that firm expectation of systematic order which rendered possible the birth of modern science. Men became scientific because they expected Law in Nature, and they expected Law in Nature because they believed in a Legislator. In most modern scientists this belief has died: it will be interesting to see how long their confidence in uniformity survives it. Two significant developments have already appeared — the hypothesis of a lawless sub-nature, and the surrender of the claim that science is true. We may be nearer than we suppose to the end of the "Scientific Age".

The Grand Miracle, says C. S. Lewis, is the Incarnation. The central miracle asserted by Christians is that God became a Man. Every other miracle prepares for this, or exhibits this, or results from this. Miracles of the Old Creation prepared for God becoming Man in Jesus Christ. Humanity, born on His shoulders, passes with Him from the cold dark water into the green warm water and out at last into the sunlight and the air.

There are Miracles of the Old Creation, and miracles of the New Creation. The latter are the miracles of the New Testament, and cannot be considered apart from the Resurrection and Ascension. The first fact in the history of Christendom is a number of people who say they have seen the Resurrection. What they bore witness to was not the action of rising from the dead but the state of having risen.

We expect the witnesses to tell of a risen life which is purely "spiritual" in the negative sense of the word. We mean a life without space, without history, without environment, with no sensuous elements in it. We also, in our heart of hearts, tend to slur over the risen *manhood* of Jesus, to conceive Him, after death, simply returning into Deity, so that the Resurrection would be no more than the reversal or undoing of the Incarnation. That being so, all references to the risen *body* make us uneasy.

It is at this point that awe and trembling fall upon us as we read the records. If the story is false, it is at least a much stranger story than we expected, something for which philosophical "religion", physical research and popular superstition have alike failed to prepare us. If the story is true, then a wholly new mode of being has arisen in the universe.

In the Walking on the Water we see the relations of spirit and nature so altered that Nature can be made to do whatever spirit pleases. This new obedience of Nature is, of course, not to be separated even in thought from spirit's own obedience to the Father of spirits. The evil reality of lawless applied science (which is Magic's son and heir) is actually reducing large tracts of Nature to disorder and sterility at this very moment.[1]

The raising of Lazarus differs from the Resurrection of Christ Himself because Lazarus, so far as we know, was not raised to a new and more glorious mode of existence but merely restored to the sort of life he had before. The fitness of the Miracle lies in the fact that He who will raise all men at the general resurrection here does it small and close, and in an inferior — a merely anticipatory — fashion.

[1] The book "Miracles" was written during the 1939-45 War.

There is more in the book "Miracles" which I could mention here, but possibly I have said enough for the reader to consider obtaining the original work, by C. S. Lewis.

I have named this chapter "Thoughts for Today". Perhaps I may conclude it with some paragraphs based on part of a shorter book which I published some three years ago.

We find ourselves in a world today which is divided into what are known as East and West, or the Eastern Bloc and the Western Bloc. Besides these two opposing blocks, which are based on Capitalism and Marxism respectively, there is a Third World, generally poorer and less developed than East and West, which tries to keep itself more or less neutral between the two opposing blocs.

I of course am a resident of the West, having been brought up in Scotland and England although I have travelled to both the United States and the Soviet Union.

I think there is a tendency, in Britain and the U.S.A., to assume, at least in official circles, that Capitalism is best and that in any conflict between East and West the capitalist West is almost certain to triumph.

In my view this is far from being the case. Without the need for a war at all, the Communist/Socialist East may quite likely triumph over the capitalist West. And the third "neutral" World, far from being well-disposed on the whole to the West, is on the whole probably more disposed towards East than West. I understand that in some African countries the bourgeois "Mr." is being replaced by "Comrade", so that "Mr." is often changed to "Cmr."

Communist and Soviet plans for opposing and eventually replacing the West probably do not include any need for a war at all. What Americans call the "domino" effect, toppling Governments in one country after another, is one part of it. Either democratic machinery or force can be used as seems most suitable. A major war is to be avoided as far as possible, but if it occurs then the East does its best to be ready for it.

If circumstances lead to war, or if the West forces war on the East, then the East considers it has a good chance of not losing (in present-day circumstances a major war which both sides would effectively lose is at least as likely as any other result). The East has much larger conventional forces than the West, and it is quite possible that a conventional war rather than an atomic war would in fact be fought. In submarines the

East is probably superior to the West — at any rate the United States is extremely worried that that may be so.

The greater part of the world's population is committed to neither the Eastern or Western alliance, but rather calls itself "the non-aligned nations". There are said to be one hundred and one of these, many of them inclined somewhat to Western or Eastern camp.

I think I have said enough to explain my view that conflict between East and West (there are various forms it can or could take) has an unpredictable result. An Eastern Bloc victory is by no means impossible, though in my view it could well be followed by some kind of Second Coming or intervention by God himself with his forces. The Apocalyptic view and prophetic writings of the past seem to me to point to this, even possibly some two thousand years after Christ's birth.

The best way to prevent the terrible immediate future which I foresee might be to improve our ways and reduce the enormous burden of evil which I see in the world and which is so strong in humanity whether East or West. Of course trying to bring about a more peaceful future by diplomatic means is to be commended and in the right circumstances might achieve a great deal.

The West, particularly the Anglo-American West, should I think be more sympathetic to the non-English speaking peoples, studying them and trying to understand them and their languages.

The East should I think make more provision for the possibility that God and religious forces may exist and have more importance than they officially maintain.

Both sides could well lose ultimately from the outbreak of a Third World War. The Nuclear Arms Race which has started is a dangerous sign of the times. The present-day balance of world power could be greatly upset and altered in the future, with or without great wars.

The suffering and backwardness of the Third World should somehow be changed for the better, so that these countries may become more prosperous and able to make the best of their potential.

One of the world's problems is the continuing increase of human population. Some efforts are being made to deal with this, but to a greater or lesser extent in different parts of the world the problem continues to increase.

To most of us the larger world problems, some of which I have mentioned, seem remote and unconnected with our own lives. There is some truth in this, but I maintain that at all levels of human relations there is a need for greater sympathy and understanding, a need for willingness to co-operate where necessary and a need to make effort to realise whatever potential we each one of us have.

2

An Earlier Life

I was born on 15th December, 1920 at Ayr, a seaside resort and County Town on the West coast of Scotland. My father was a Forestry Commission District Officer and both he and my mother came from land-owning families whose country estates were situated on the outer margins of the broad and fertile acres of Central Ayrshire.

By the time I was five we were living at Ayr in a house with a large garden on a road leading down to the sandy sea shore. I had a younger brother and played happily with him and the children from a neighbouring house who came through a gate in the wall separating the two gardens. My childhood was happy.

When I was six I remember attending the christening of my youngest brother which was performed by a minister who came into Ayr from Straiton, the parish where my father and grandfather's estate was. I remember about this time too seeing many children with coloured blazers cycling along the main road near our house, on their way to Ayr Academy. I thought to myself that if all went well, I too would one day be a boy riding his bicycle to the Academy.

This indeed was not to be. When I was seven, my father resigned from the Forestry Commission, in order to move into the large mansion on his father's estate and plant trees there instead of on Forestry Commission land. The house, which had been let to a retired General, was said to be in a bad state. Certainly the next year was taken up with moving and decorating on a grand scale.

The move from Ayr to Blairquhan, the name of the house, did not meet with my approval. Indeed ever since then (unlike my

16

two brothers) I have been as happy to live in a town as in the country. In fact, I would rather be "shut up" in a town than cut off in some remote countryside.

My father was nephew to three bachelor uncles living in the London area, all of whom were wealthy and one, a retired Director

My parents' wedding in London 1917.

17

My brother David and myself (right) at our house in Ayr, 1927.

of a well-known merchant bank, particularly so. They interested themselves in my education, and it was decided that I should go as a boarder to a privately-owned "preparatory" school near London.

I remember the preparations, the buying and fitting of strange clothes for me. I set off on a four hundred mile train journey and eventually arrived at the school in a kind of miniature plus-four suit which was then in fashion at such places.

There were nine "new boys" that term, two of whom it was thought might well obtain public-school scholarships later. I was one of the two. I remember there being pointed out to me Lord Lascelles, a relative of the King, and the two sons of the Duke of Devonshire who seemed to be called Burlington and Cavendish.

The first term seemed to pass pleasantly enough, and I was glad to be home for Christmas. Next term was the dreaded Easter Term, when it was usual for boys to be ill and often games and matches were not able to be played.

This particular Easter Term was worse than most. A poisonous germ in the throat, causing what was called a Streptococcal infection, affected many of the boys. Six of them died from it and the school was eventually moved to a new and apparently more healthy site in Berkshire.

Meanwhile I was suffering from the disease. My throat became completely blocked. The doctors decided to cut a hole in my trachea below the chin so that I was able to breathe through a tube which ran from my mouth to the trachea. I had three or four operations altogether, as the doctors tried to clear up the septic condition in my neck by cutting holes in it.

In the 1914-18 war my mother had been a Red Cross nurse. She took to the sick bed atmosphere like a duck to water and organized for a time four nurses for me at once (two day nurses and two night nurses). The tube I was breathing through quickly became blocked so I would make a faint sound and a nurse would clear it by some means or other. My temperature rose I think to 108°F, but after six weeks I was in the process of recovering. I am still lucky to have a strong constitution.

As I began to recover, I would ask permission to get out of bed and walk. Whether or not the permission was granted, I did walk, and as a result began to have a series of heart attacks. I was taken to convalesce at home and with various relatives, but it was more than two years (by which time I was eleven) before I could be said to have recovered from the illness.

My mother was very displeased with the school at which the

epidemic had taken place so it was resolved that my brothers, and myself eventually would go to a different "preparatory" school. While lying on my back after the heart attacks, growing both tall and fat, I passed my time reading enormous quantities of literature. A favourite was Arthur Mee's Children's Encyclopaedia, in twelve volumes, which I devoured from cover to cover. I was an addict of his "Children's Newspaper" too. Later I was at the village "Public" school at Straiton, Ayrshire, for about a year.

When I finally returned to boarding school life, at a different school, at the age of eleven, I could be described as something of an eccentric. Tall, ungainly, clumsy and fat, my school nick-name was "Monster". I could name every country in the world with its capital and other features (I collected stamps) but when it came to playing games, which in smart circles was considered more important in those days, I did not shine.

My educational career took me next to the celebrated Eton College, Windsor, in 1933. My intended house-master, Mr Howson, had been killed with several other Eton masters in a climbing accident in the Alps the previous winter; so I found myself instead with Mr Routh, a teacher of English whose special knowledge was the works and life of William Shakespeare.

House-masters in those days were very much lords and masters of their houses, except that if they were bachelors they had perhaps some competition to face in the Dame (her position is called Matron in most schools) and this I was to find in my time at Routh's House. Mr Routh was very much an Englishman (he later became Curator of the Shakespeare Museum at Stratford) and the Matron, Miss Joan Owen, was I believe Welsh. I do not think that either had spent much time in Scotland, and I am sure they never expressed a wish to go there.

My education, and my life generally, continued to progress in a series of "fits and starts." Never quite in the top form, I often did well in exams., and collected a moderate number of prizes. I enjoyed studying languages like French and Ancient Greek. One hobby on which I spent much time was finding out all I could about the extensive French colonies in Africa and elsewhere, a subject on which I have never encountered anything but absolute ignorance among British people in almost every walk of life.

Another hobby I took up at school was studying railways and their timetables. I was able to go by train to attend the annual Rowing Regatta at Henley.

I also joined a school excursion to visit the Great Western

Railway works at Swindon, where I took a photograph of a middle-aged gentleman working at a lathe. He enjoyed talking to me, gave me his address and I promised to send him his photograph. Possibly because I lost his address, I never did so and the thought gave me an unpleasant feeling of shame and dishonesty for many years afterwards.

It was considered important that all boys should take part in some sporting activities. I chose rowing because, although very strenuous for short periods, it seemed to offer the best opportunities for vanishing up the River Thames away from the school and in general the pleasant moments were not too much out of proportion to the unpleasant ones.

During their last few terms at school most boys became "specialists" of one kind or another. I chose to become a Language Specialist, a status which I only enjoyed for two or three terms before leaving the school in the year 1938. Language specialists were regarded on the whole as eccentric. The general level achieved in French, the only foreign language taught at most British schools, can at Eton as elsewhere only be described as poor.

Before I left school, arrangements had to be made for my further activities. My father, who achieved a high level of scholarship in Latin and Greek during his school days, at Wellington College, had gone on to Balliol College, Oxford, and achieved a fairly good degree in Classics there. It was agreed that my level of scholarship was sufficient for me to sit the entrance examination to this College — renowned as a centre of "Plain Living and High Thinking," as I was frequently told later — in the summer.

My days spent at Balliol College sitting the entrance exam, were rewarded with success. I became due to enter Oxford as a Freshman in October, 1939. On leaving school in December, 1938, I found myself with nine months to spend more or less according to my own inclinations.

I got a letter during the summer holidays of 1938 from a school friend John Ponsonby, inviting me to join him and Vicary Gibbs in a safari trip through Central Africa where the Gibbs family had plantations and other business interests. I considered this offer, but decided to carry on with my previous plan to study the French language and way of life, in France.

So in January I set off for Aix-en-Provence where I had arranged to stay with M. Marcel Ruff, a former Eton master now teaching at Aix, who with his wife gave hospitality and tuition (at a

21

price) to young men wishing to study French to enter the Diplomatic Service or for other reasons.

I spent three months at Aix, attending some lectures at the University of Aix/Marseille and worked fairly hard with M. Ruff. I was able to join the Ski Club of Aix-en-Provence, which rolled merrily in a hired coach every weekend through the Lower Alps and the valley of a tributary of the Rhône to Alpine ski-ing grounds.

It was noticeable at that time that the French were far from being a sporting or athletic nation. The jolly skiers of Aix spent little time actually ski-ing, and what ski-ing they did was of a limited and unambitious type. The main objectives of the day were good food and drink, although to a young British man of that date the freedom with which the sexes mixed and the activities in which they indulged were also noticeable.

At the end of three months I decided I wanted to go and study in Paris, and actually sit an exam. at a French University. It was arranged by M. Ruff that I should do a holiday course lasting a month or two at the University of Paris (the Sorbonne).

I was to stay at a kind of boarding house kept by a friend of the Ruffs, Madame Martin, and her daughter Marietta.

In April, 1939, I duly arrived 'chez Madame Martin' at a fairly modest house with small garden in the smart Paris 16th District of Passy. I discovered that to get to the course I was to follow at the University I had to go right across the centre of Paris, a distance of several miles. Before long I found that the best way to do this was to take a bus, the AX.

The course for which I was enrolled was a 'Cours de Vacance pour les Étrangers'. It filled several large classrooms with a noisy crowd of young people, most of whom resided just outside Paris at the Cité Universitaire. An impressive babble in French, English, Spanish, Vietnamese, Japanese, and many other languages filled the air. At first a bit startled by my surroundings, I was before long taking it all for granted.

Life at the pension kept by Mme. Martin and her daughter was comparatively quiet. Another resident there was a smallish, fairly dark Italian girl called Bettina Vegara. I decided that I would attempt a sexual conquest of her.

At this time I was aged eighteen, and I had decided that the British young men of my acquaintance were behindhand compared with other countries in their relations with the opposite sex. I must confess too that I was beginning to wonder whether I personally was well endowed with sex appeal. I had every intention of finding out.

The young ladies of the University, with their garish clothes and loud fierce conversations, certainly had a frightening effect on me. I could not see myself in an intimate relation with any of them.

Marietta Martin seemed to be aged about thirty. She was pale, thin and extremely learned. She had been a lot in Poland, and had published a book called 'Une Française à Varsovie'. She and her mother seemed to be very devout Catholics. (Marietta Martin later became a "Heroine of the Resistance" during the German Occupation, and there is a plaque at what was their house at Passy to record this).

I did my best to open a conversation with Bettina. Before long it seemed that French was the best language, although my French had not yet acquired the fluency which it has today. But try as I might, I could not raise more than an attitude of smiling condescension in Bettina, a most self-contained young woman perhaps three years older than me. After a few weeks my attempts at seduction were indefinitely postponed.

But my studies at the University proceeded fairly well. We heard lectures from two professors, Professor Michaud and Professor Georgin. We did a certain amount of written work, and it began to emerge that my marks were very much nearer the top of the class than the bottom. I got into the way, with or without companions, of having fairly cheap lunches in the Boulevard Saint-Michel. I explored Nôtre Dame cathedral, and at the weekends made one or two excursions to the stunningly beautiful cathedral at Chartres. Another excursion was to the celebrated former nunnery at Port-Royal-des-Champs.

A well-known place to go with a girl or boy friend in Paris, or to meet one of the opposite sex — was the Luxembourg Gardens, still much the same today. Seated on a bench there one day I began talking to a young Belgian girl at the other end of the seat. She was not specially beautiful, with hair that could be called mouse-coloured. However, I am glad to say that she responded to my advances. We became good friends and had many meals together. As far as I can remember she was a devout Catholic, and guarded her virtue with religious devotion. When I finally returned to Britain she actually wrote to me, but I was not over-interested and the relationship in the end faded away.

On balance I can say that I enjoyed my time in Paris very

much. When I came to take my exam. at the University, I got "very good" marks in Literature, History, Grammar and Lexicology and "mediocre" marks in a peculiar French institution called "Explication de Textes." I was awarded a Certificate after Examination (First Class) of the University of Paris, which has been of considerable value to me many times since.

Before I start on my Oxford University career, it may be of interest to say something about the life I led during the holidays from school. My mother took part with great enthusiasm in Ayrshire Society. I was fond of my mother (as she was of me) and I followed her comings and goings in the local Society with, perhaps, more enthusiasm than wisdom.

My father, I may say, was at that time renowned for the fact that he did not conform with what local Society demanded of him. At the Ayr race meetings, which could be very smart indeed, he wore an old dark blue suit of his youth which gradually turned green with the passing of the years. He took a pride in wearing his ties until they fell to pieces and became unusable.

My mother saw that I took part in everything that the smart set in Ayr and district could provide. Not for nothing was Ayrshire known in some circles as Millionaire-shire. Many who had made fortunes in coal, iron, shipping, stock-broking or other activities (usually in Glasgow or Central Scotland) bought mansions in Ayrshire. My maternal grandfather, who founded a Glasgow ship-owning firm, and became a Director of the Glasgow and South-Western Railway, was one of these.

As a boy I was sent to Miss Webster's dancing class in Ayr. Although invariably in the second row rather than the first, I at least met many of the "young ladies and gentlemen" who would be worth knowing in later years. Unfortunately, from my point of view, Ayrshire suffered and still suffers from the fact that at every level of society it produces — or appeared to produce — some four boys to every three girls. It has always been one of my ambitions (so far unrealized) to find myself in a society where there were twelve girls to every boy.

My mother was a keen rider, and had supported the local Eglinton Hunt. I was persuaded, to my complete lack of enjoyment, from time to time to ride a horse. My father's family were in fact notorious for not liking horses, and I can still see my father's face as he stood by with a sardonic expression

24

waiting for one of his sons, or his wife, to fall off a horse.

Another diversion of Ayrshire society was tennis parties. I am glad to say that my tennis was definitely better than my golf, so that I was able to take part in a fair number of tennis parties. There again the girls I fancied for their beauty or intelligence were usually carried off by more handsome and/or intelligent young men, and I was usually left at best with girls whom I considered to be in the second rank for beauty and/or intellect.

While I and my friends were disporting ourselves at tennis, racing, shooting and other activities, the clouds of war were boiling up with a vengeance. In September, 1939, Britain declared war on Germany and shortly after we were informed that some forty evacuees were to arrive in a few days at Blairquhan, the mansion where my parents resided and managed the mansion and Estate.

Sure enough, the evacuees did arrive and my mother took charge with her usual enthusiasm and organizing ability. My father, I think, retired into his study and was hardly seen at all. My mother was fairly soon appointed Commandant of the 64th Ayrshire Red Cross Detachment. My father, after he had spent a few months considering the situation, emerged and before long became a leading light in the local aircraft observing centre of the Royal Observer Corps.

My arrival at Oxford University in October seemed to mark a joining place between the old nineteenth century Oxford and the new twentieth century Oxford which began with the outbreak of war in 1939.

We were shown to our rooms up the neo-Gothic 19th century staircases of Balliol College (in fact parts of the college are considerably older than nineteenth century). It had been solemnly explained to us that each gentleman usually had two rooms, a bedroom and a study, but that owing to the war each pair of rooms were to be shared between two gentlemen.

I met my fellow-gentleman, a dark rather intense Welshman named Brian Lloyd who wore a long scholar's gown which showed that he had won a Balliol scholarship. We engaged in conversation. He said he would be doing Science, and I said that I hoped to be reading Philosophy, Politics and Economics.

He suggested that if we shared the bedroom, the study would be more free for work and/or entertaining. I agreed.

Before long we were assembled outside the College Hall to have our photograph taken. Inside the hall we were given a talk by the Master of Balliol which elaborated on the theme of "plain living and high thinking" which I had already heard mentioned quite a number of times.

We had by now been shown the toilets and bathrooms which were completely inadequate in number. After dinner in the Hall we were left to our own devices and it appeared to be the done thing to assemble under the wall which we shared with Trinity College next door. Insults were nightly shouted over the wall, of which the most common was "Bloody Trinity! Bloody Trinity!" Trinity did not always deign to reply, but when they did they had what they thought was a trump card. Balliol had a reputation, well founded, for having at least one black man among its numbers for many years past. "Bring out your black man, Balliol" was the cry from Trinity.

I was told of one celebrated occasion when a black man managed to get past the stern defences of Trinity and enter the College. "Bring out your black man, Trinity!" shouted Balliol with glee. Trinity bore it for a while, then some Trinity wit came out with the answer. "Bring our your white man, Balliol" rang out across the darkened quadrangles.

Brian Lloyd and I had many long and intellectual discussions about Science and the Arts, being Scottish and being Welsh, joining the Forces and fighting wars, (Brian believed in non-violence) and many other subjects. We became good friends, and shared rooms for over a year.

A common phrase of the time was "there's a war on." Because of the war a special form of Degree was devised for those going into the Forces. You did what was called a "Section" (a Section was an exam. in what was normally a small part of a subject). If you passed three Section exams., and did sufficient war service to bring the total time up to three years, you got a B.A. degree.

It was my intention to go into the Army after four terms at Oxford, but I did not look forward to the Army with any great pleasure. I had been a rather clumsy Cadet, bad at drill, in the Officers' Training Corps at Eton. However I had obtained my Certificate A in military studies, which meant that I would be treated as a Potential Officer when I was called up into the Army.

It was possible to join the Oxford University Officers'

Training Corps, which meant more drill and military studies and the possibility of obtaining Army Certificate 'B' which meant that I would proceed directly when called up to an Officer Cadet Training Unit without having to pass through the ranks as a Potential Officer. However, influenced perhaps by Brian Lloyd, I decided not to join the O.T.C. while at Oxford.

My Oxford studies proceeded fairly well. Balliol, a large and intellectual college, was able to provide tutors in almost any subject. I did Politics and Economics — it was thought I think that we could hardly make sufficient progress in Philosophy to justify our studying it in the four terms available. Instead of Philosophy, we were persuaded to do a Section in History. In both Oxford and Cambridge, a study of English political history from the sixteenth to nineteenth centuries seems to be the standard subject for those otherwise uncertain what to do.

My four terms at Oxford passed all too quickly. Apart from the black-out, rationing and so on the war was not too much in evidence, it being the period of the so-called "Phoney-war." In 1940 the German Invasion of France took place. In December of that year I left Balliol and in January 1941, I was "Called to the Colours" with the King's Own Yorkshire Light Infantry at a camp near York.

I discovered afterwards that there were no facilities whatever for the training of Potential Officers, or Officer Cadets, in Scotland. All Scottish Potential Officers were called up to the K.O.Y.L.I. at York.

In January, 1941, I made my way to York and reported at the Infantry Training Centre there. As I expected, the experience was not pleasant. There were various innoculations against infectious diseases and we spent much of the first few days in the Barrack Room. The Potential Officers, mostly from the North of England, were a varied but interesting set of people. The rest of the recruits appeared to me to have come from the slums of Yorkshire towns (Pontefract, Tadcaster, Doncaster, or Ponty, Taddy and Donny as the lads called them).

I had come face to face with the phenomenon of Two Nations which struck many other people, both writers and non-writers, for the first time during the war. Whereas the so-called Potential Officer types tended to be fairly tall, well-educated and have most of their teeth, the others were smaller, illiterate and badly-spoken and tended to have lost most of their teeth. Most of the P.O. types had hardly encountered the "other Nation" types before, and it was something of an eye-opener to them.

As I had feared, I stood out for being bad at drill, being caught out at kit inspections and badly turned out in my uniform. I thought about an idea I had before joining the Army; I wanted to do Intelligence work.

One day I applied to see the Colonel, and told him I wanted to go in for Intelligence. "You mean you want to join the Intelligence Corps" he said. "Yes," I agreed, never having heard of the Intelligence Corps before. "Do you want to become an officer first or do you want a transfer to the Intelligence Corps?" he asked. "I believe they are all Lance-Corporals at least in the I.C." I said I would like a transfer to the Intelligence Corps. "Very well, Hunter-Blair" said the Colonel.

After a further period of "square bashing," as it was called, my transfer to the I.C. came through. I received a railway warrant to a town in Hampshire and made my way there, taking care not to fall foul of "Red-caps," (military policemen) and "R.T.O.'s" (Railway Transport Officers) on the way.

The Intelligence Corps depot, on the edge of an old town, made a pleasant first impression. I was pleased to find myself in a barrack-room filled with very much the same type of Potential Officer person as I had left behind at York, although now the average age of the Hampshire types was well above my age. Many of them were sergeants, corporals and lance-corporals. A high proportion seemed to have been schoolmasters in civilian life.

It took me a day or so to settle down in this new regiment. I tried to make some inquiries about what we were going to do and what sort of training we were going to get. "You want to know about the I.C.?" said one. "Do you know what its cap badge is?" I confessed that I did not know. "Officially it is a rose resting on a laurel wreath, but some people say it is a pansy resting on its laurels!"

I made myself a friend in Lance-Corporal Pendlebury. He was a fair-haired, lanky, young man from Lancashire, who had been a schoolmaster at a boys' "preparatory" school before joining the Army. From him and others, I learnt that we were to have training in motor-cycle despatch riding, revolver-shooting and a certain amount of general intelligence work.

Soon I was getting into the routine of life at the I.C. depot. There was a certain amount of drill, but not very much. On about the second night, I was astounded to hear what seemed to be bird music more beautiful than I could have imagined. I listened to the warbling notes for a while, and later (was it next morning?) I asked "what was that remarkable bird music I heard during the night?" "Don't you know, that's a nightingale." It took me a little while to believe what I was told. Certainly I had never before heard a nightingale sing, which I believe in Britain is heard only a few months of the year, mainly in the counties which border the English Channel.

I made some progress at Intelligence work, including the motor-cycle and revolver shooting, but I still had trouble in looking smart in my uniform, and in getting through drill tests and kit inspections.

Finally, after about two months, I was called to see my new Colonel. He told me that he had been thinking about me, and had come to the conclusion that my best future probably did not lie in an Army career. I was to see a doctor (or was it a psychiatrist?) in the celebrated Army hospital of Netley.

Soon my appointment came through to go to Netley. I made my way to this large, low hospital, where every room seemed to have a large verandah. Someone told me later that the plans for building a hospital in India had been used to build Netley, with the result that the building has a wide-open, tropical appearance. There I saw my "trick-cyclist," as the slang expression has it, and was told that a report would be sent to my Commanding Officer.

As sometimes happens in Army circles, I was able to look through my own papers at a later date, thanks to the help of a friendly clerk. There I saw the Army psychiatrist's report, which seemed to confirm what the Colonel has said about my being more suited to civilian life. I am told that part of the secret of being a good Army doctor is putting in reports that agree with what the Colonel thinks. At all events, I was R.T.U.ed (returned to unit) which is something of a disgrace in Army life.

So I found myself back at York, but this time no longer a Potential Officer. In fact, the authorities in my old regiment really did not know what to do with me, and I was more or less excused all training and exercises. I consoled myself by spending a lot of time in the camp kitchen, where I was given chips and other culinary gifts by friendly A.T.S. girls. I have a photo of an A.T.S. girl in the K.O.Y.L.I. kitchen which I took at this time.

After a few weeks, further instructions came through (from the War office, perhaps?) about me. I was to be discharged from the Army and return to civilian life, probably to Oxford University as I had told people that my studies there were not complete. I went through the formalities of handing in my rifle and kit, and was given a Discharge Certificate detailing my Army service and including a testimonial to me as "sober, honest and a willing worker."

After returning home at His Majesty's expense in September, 1941, I wrote to Balliol College, Oxford, and asked if I could resume my studies there. They agreed to this.

When I returned to Oxford in October, I found myself in rather a curious position. As I had already qualified in the examinations for my War Degree (Bachelor of Arts) all that was needed for me to obtain the degree was for me to complete a total of approved study and/or war service.

I decided to take advantage of this state of affairs to embark on a further study of languages, a subject in which I have always been interested. There was a feeling abroad in Britain at that time that the country had a great need of Russian linguists. The Soviet Union were by that time our Allies, and being hard pressed by the enemy (mainly Germans) public opinion in Britain was all in favour of helping the Russians and the idea was put about, both in and out of official circles, that provision of greatest possible help was held up by a shortage of Russian linguists on the British side.

When I made enquiries at Balliol College about the possibility of studying Russian, I found my way made very easy. A Senior Don at the College, Humphrey Sumner, was more or less in charge of Russian studies. He was willing to give me some instruction himself and he also put me in touch with what seemed to me and everyone else a most glamorous figure, a tall, heavy bear-like Russian named Sergei Konovalov.

As a pass in Russian would only amount to one subject. I was told that I should also do another subject, and German was recommended. I agreed to this. So far as I can remember my instructors in German were mainly middle-aged ladies from Womens' Colleges.

I can hardly remember whether I ever did take any

exams in Russian and German, for of course they were not required for my degree. At all events I completed my studies in the languages in June, 1942, and graduated (without much ceremony) Bachelor of Arts.

My year at Oxford was darkened by the fact that in May, 1942, the Master of the College called on me to tell me that my second brother, David, had been killed as a Pilot Officer soon after training in Oklahoma, U.S.A., to fly Spitfires with the Royal Air Force. In fact I got into rather a depressing routine of lying in fairly late in the morning, not doing very much except perhaps reading, and going to bed fairly late at night. I was friendly for a time with a girl called Marigold Phillips, whom I found most attractive — but my thoughts while with her were usually "What have I, with my uncertain future, got to offer a nice girl like Marigold?" Indeed I would be glad to know what has happened to her in the years that have passed since then. (I have since been in touch with Marigold, and her life after Oxford seems to have been almost as varied as mine).

At the suggestion of the Master of Balliol College, I was put in touch with the Iona Community, which did religious and social work in Glasgow and Edinburgh, and whose members spend (and still spend) the summer months on the island of Iona, where they have re-built the ancient Cathedral of the Isles. After some correspondence in which I and senior members of the College took part, it was arranged that I should stay for most of the month of August with the Iona Community at Iona in the Western Isles of Scotland.

After this stretch of time what I remember most clearly about Iona is the long and bumpy bus journey along bad roads on the island of Mull which was necessary for taking a small boat from the end of Mull across the Sound of Iona, which was a few hundred yards wide.

I remember that I helped the masons in their building work on the former Abbey and Cathedral, which are now completed and a tremendous tourist attraction to visitors from every part of the world. The Community had and has its own living quarters, where adequate meals are enjoyed in the midst of a fairly austere life of prayers, work and church service. The Leader of the Community, the Rev Dr George McLeod, had the reputation of being a Socialist which in those days was enough to condemn him in the eyes of most of the Conservatives and upper-class people whom my family regarded as equals.

In my spare time I explored the island of Iona, and managed to make friends with a young man named MacLeod who was a student at Glasgow University. I told him I thought I would go and start work of some kind in Glasgow the next month, September, and he gave me the address of his lodgings at Elderslie Street, Hillhead, near the University.

After some three weeks with the Iona Community (I believe they and I found each other congenial) I went home to Ayrshire and then up to Glasgow where I moved into Kenneth MacLeod's lodgings. After a day or so I went down to the labour exchange, and they found me a post with Pickford's furniture removal and storage and travel service.

This was really the first time I had taken up regular employment (apart from the Army) and I found it interesting enough. In fact town life had a real appeal for me — perhaps it reminded me of my first seven years in Ayr before I was pulled away into the countryside. The staff at Pickford's interested me, and should I say that I interested them as a well-spoken, well educated member of the upper class. There was not the same ill-feeling on the part of the workers against the middle and upper classes that there is today. Among Scottish people in particular (perhaps not so much in England) there was a readiness to extend the hand of friendship to all neighbours whoever they might be.

I went round Glasgow making lists of furniture of households who wanted to move, and eventually I was able to give an estimate for the more ordinary sort of removal myself. On a few occasions I tried my hand out with the removal men actually shifting the furniture. Perhaps it was at that time that I decided that heavy manual labour of any kind was not a life that I would choose other than on a very short-term basis, but I still remember the foreman, Mr McGuire, whom I liked most on the staff of Messrs Pickford, Glasgow Branch.

In December, 1942, I obtained a position with the Western Motor Company, who were engaged on war work making shell cases and the like. I was put in the Progress Department whose duty was to go round from machinist to machinist seeing that the work was completed and transferred to the next machinist on the production line. Sometimes we were called "progress chasers," and we were sometimes unpopular with some of the shop floor people. I am sure I preferred being in the Progress Department to being a permanent machinist, as I would say that I have always preferred movement and activity to any fixed and immobile job. "Movement is Life" was the motto of the Women's League of Health and Beauty, to which my mother belonged, and I would agree with that.

My period with Western Motors, Glasgow, only lasted about a month as in January, 1943, the Appointments Department of the Ministry of Labour offered me a post in the Postal and Telegraph Censorship as a Grade 1 Examiner with special foreign language qualifications.

I was told that the work was very confidential, and that it was to be in London. If anybody asked what I was doing, I was to say that I was working with the Ministry of Information.

At the end of January I made my way to London and reported for duty in a building next the Post Office Headquarters.

I found I was part of a Russian Language Section, whose duty would be to act as censors on a telephone link which was to be set up between London and Moscow. People told me that this project had been underway for several months and that little progress was being made. In fact, it turned out that the proposed telephone link was never set up and the purpose for which the three telephone censors had been recruited never came into existence.

The three members of the Russian Section were a Mrs Fürst, a youngish lady who had been born in Leningrad and had married George Fürst, a Jewish businessman in North London; Mr Fedorov, who was always very mysterious and would not tell you anything about his past background; and myself.

Looking at the matter again many years after the war, and with the benefit of my added knowledge and experience, it seems fairly clear to me that Mrs Fürst and myself were appointed by the British Authorities, and that Mr Fedorov was probably appointed by the Soviet Authorities or the Soviet Embassy. It seems strange now that none of us ever thought of this at the time. Mr Fedorov must have been instructed not to let on that he was, in fact, a Soviet national and as a result he decided to say the very least possible about himself. We found him quite pleasant, but aloof.

The main activity in the building where we were was censoring British Inland telephone communications, which was done in the main by people who could only speak English.

There was a Welsh lady who, I think, had been appointed to censor any telephone conversation in Welsh. Indeed, she worked mainly on the London-Cardiff telephone circuit, but like us all she was free to listen in on any of a large proportion of the long distance telephone calls in the United Kingdom.

The International censors, of whom I was one, were called Grade 1 Examiners and the others may have been Grade II although I am not sure of this. The International Censors censored the telephone line between Britain and the United States, which was fairly busy with frequent official calls between officials in London and Washington, often at the very highest level.

The censor was able to speak to the people engaged on the call, and before it started we read over a little warning that the line might be intercepted by the enemy, and that the greatest care should be exercised. If we thought that the caller was being indiscreet, we were able to cut into the conversation or cut off the call. From the information I gathered, neither Winston Churchill nor President Roosevelt had been cut off in mid-call by a British examiner.

There was also a telephone circuit between London and Geneva, which was used for discussing exchanges of prisoners of war and for dealing with Red Cross matters, like sending parcels to prisoners of war. Those working on this circuit were supposed to be French speakers. People on the international circuit or Russian circuit who knew French could do this duty which involved, sometimes, talking to telephone operators in Geneva or censoring conversations in French.

I found this work rather interesting at first, but eventually it became somewhat tedious, particularly as the Russian circuit did not open. The V1 attacks on London came while I was engaged on this work, but did not have as much effect as the original London Blitz had.

I was, in fact about 22 years of age, and eventually found myself in the middle of an affaire with one of the other telephone examiners as we were called. She had never got on particularly well with her husband, and when he was called up she was quite lonely in her house in the London suburbs and I regret to say I was quite happy to end her loneliness. This affaire lasted quite a long time, her husband being a very unsuspecting person who perhaps was not interested in the sexual side of marriage. When he was on leave we used to go about in a threesome, having drinks in pubs and sometimes making trips into the countryside. I can remember one occasion when the husband got lost during a weekend, in a public house, and we were able to take advantage of his absence. When he finally returned he did not appear to notice that his wife and I were on what I thought were obviously intimate terms.

About two years before the end of the war, the higher authorities evidently decided that the need for censorship had become less urgent. The staff of the Postal and Telegraph Censorship Department began to be run down, and we all started to wonder how much longer we would hold our jobs.

At this time, a friend asked me if I would be interested in newspaper work, as she was friendly with the secretary of Lord Rothermere, owner of the Daily Mail. Eager to "try anything once," I said I was interested in working on a newspaper, and I was introduced to Lord Rothermere's secretary and her husband. I became friendly with them. It was suggested that the secretary could mention my name to Lord Rothermere in his office in the Daily Mail building just off Fleet Street. About this time I had been told that my censorship post would shortly come to an end, so I was all the more keen to get into journalism.

After a while the word came from Lord Rothermere (who interviewed me in his office) that he did not particularly want me to join the Daily Mail staff, but if I liked I could see the Editor of the Evening News, a London evening newspaper which proudly proclaimed every day that it had "the World's Largest Evening Net Sale"; so I saw Mr Guy Schofield, the Editor, who said I could join the paper on a trial basis as a reporter and possibly do other jobs, besides reporting, as well.

Not long after that I started work with the London Evening News. I found that nearly all the staff reported for work at 8 o'clock in the morning, with a few starting at 7 or even 6 a.m. At that time I was living in Chiswick, and I cannot say that I ever found it a pleasant or easy task to get to work just off Fleet Street at times varying from 6 to 8 in the morning.

My first instruction was to go into the Reporters' Room and learn to type, so I pounded away on a typewriter and bought a book on typing to help me. I never used more than two fingers in principle, but nevertheless was able to get up to the quite good speed of 40 words per minute. I was also advised to learn shorthand, but told this was not essential. As it turned out I invented my own shorthand, a kind of abbreviation of words in longhand where once again I was able to get up to quite a good speed though not fast enough to take down the words of a fast speaker as he was speaking.

At first, I was told I was not a very good reporter, and that I had a lot to learn. After a time I was sent into the News Room, where I put on earphones and wrote down the words of reporters who rang up over the telephones. This I managed to do with some success, although I was not allowed to put down the words of the fastest speaking and/or most highly regarded of the reporters.

After a spell in the News Room, I began to wonder how soon I could find a way to get out of it. The atmosphere of heavy old typewriters, of large mugs of tea, of ambitious Cockney lads with whom I did not have much in common, I did not much enjoy. The News Editor was a fearsome man of Danish origin who boomed and shouted in a loud voice all over the room, and on frequent occasions could give a reporter or telephonist a most unpleasant ticking off.

After a while, I summoned courage to go and see Guy Schofield, the editor, who was a gentle religious man who wrote books about Christianity and the Holy Land for children and adults. Because he was liable to be imposed upon by people, he had a most fearsome secretary called Pamela who thought it was her duty to prevent as many people as possible from seeing the editor. She had an affected, stilted voice, wore a lot of makeup and was not much liked by most of the Evening News staff.

Pamela prevented me from seeing the editor for a while, but eventually I got past her at last and saw Guy Schofield. He agreed that it was time I had a change and suggested that I join the Talk of the Day Department, which was a gossip column, giving news of society events and all other kinds of personal matters in London and district.

The T.O.D. Department was presided over by a bad-tempered Irishman who was as bad as the gentleman of Danish extraction in the News Room. Charles Curran, the T.O.D. editor could be fairly pleasant but he could also be very sarcastic, cynical and even fierce. On one occasion he reduced a lady reporter to tears.

I discovered that I was better at writing a gossip column, or part of it, than I am at being an ordinary newspaper reporter. The reason may be that I think I am more interested in people than in things.

With my knowledge of languages and foreigners, I was usually the one chosen to attend Embassy parties and events of that nature, unless Mr Curran wished to attend them himself. I was also given curious tasks like interviewing the man who had the biggest collection of match box labels in London.

As well as going out on stories given us to cover by our departmental editor, we were expected to suggest suitable stories which we or another reporter would cover for the paper. I became fairly good at this, as I have always been a person with a great flow of ideas — sometimes too many for my own popularity or comfort. I would write up the stories without further enquiries where that was suitable, and they were often published. I was lucky to know a fair number of "Society" people and could give information about them. There was a big risk of making myself unpopular with my friends and relations if I gave intimate details about their lives to the Press, but I was able to hold a balance in these matters fairly well.

At one stage in my career with the Evening News I was given a radio set in a little room and told to listen to the British and foreign (including enemy) broadcasts, and told to pass on information so obtained to the paper. Apparently it was thought I might get some "scoop" or news in advance of other papers, but I do not think I ever heard anything very important of that kind.

When I had been with the Evening News for a few years, it occurred to those in charge that perhaps it would be better if the paper had a Foreign Editor who would take charge of obtaining foreign news.

It seemed strange to me that the paper had managed without a Foreign Editor and Foreign Department for such a very long time. In fact, when I had suggested that we ought to have a Foreign Editor like other papers, no one ever agreed with me. "We get our foreign news from the Agencies," they said "and in any case our readers are not interested in foreign news. This is a Londoner's paper, and the average Londoner doesn't know or care what happens in other countries or even in the more remote parts of Britain."

However it seemed this splendid insularity had to come to an end and a Foreign Editor was appointed, with me as his assistant. I used to call myself Assistant Foreign Editor, but there seemed to be some doubt as to whether that was really my title.

The Foreign Department consisting of the Foreign Editor, myself and the Diplomatic Correspondent, was given a room which we shared at first with the author of the "Courts Day by Day" column and with the artist who illustrated the daily short story. They were certainly very pleasant, rather quiet people. The author of "Courts Day by Day", James A. Jones, had achieved quite a fame for his column.

The Foreign Editor, Mr Harold Walton, was a native of Leicester who had been connected at one time with a paper called the Continental Daily Mail. It was printed in Paris, and I may say no longer exists. I think it was too British in character to appeal to the Americans in Europe. To achieve success at the present time an English language paper in Europe has to appeal both to the Americans and to the British.

Mr Walton, assisted by me, appointed a number of correspondents round the world who sent in stories in telegraphic form. I usually had the job of typing them out and submitting them in a form, which would appeal to our sub-editors. With the best will in the world, a high proportion of the foreign copy was "spiked" by the subs., who rather took the general view that the great British public wasn't interested in foreign news.

It was about this time that the war came to an end. Certainly the celebrations in London on V.E. Day and V.J. Day were tremendous occasions, which I was glad to have taken part in.

Our Foreign Department continued to make modest progress. There was a daily editorial conference in the morning, when the editor would check up on which heads of departments had actually arrived. They were supposed to give him an outline of their main news stories and plans for the day. The editorial conference ended with a general conversation.

If Mr Walton was absent, I was usually invited to attend the editorial conference in his place. Not long after the end of the war Mr Churchill, the Prime Minister, announced that there would be a General Election. The Labour and Liberal members who had been in the Cabinet left the Cabinet, and the Conservatives announced that they would carry on, on their own, until the General Election. On the morning when this happened, there was some discussion at the editorial conference as to how the news that the Conservatives were to carry on alone would be presented. I had one of my ideas, "Why not call it a Caretaker Cabinet," I ventured to say. The editor, news editor and chief sub-editor seemed to think that was a good idea and our next edition duly came out with the headlines CARETAKER CABINET FORMED.

The phrase Caretaker Cabinet was taken up by the morning papers next day, and rather gave people the impression that this Cabinet was merely a temporary pretty unimportant affair, to last until a new Government was formed after the Election. I believe Mr Churchill was disappointed with the phrase Caretaker Cabinet or Caretaker Government, as he had rather hoped people would associate the Conservatives with Victory and a successful Government.

When the General Election results finally became known, it turned out to be a great victory for Labour. Instead of thanking the Conservatives for winning the war, the great British public expressed its dislike of the officials and the officers in the Services who had ruled over them during the war. They wanted the working classes to rule through the Labour Party, and Mr Attlee was happy to take charge of this; but possibly my phrase may have helped him a little.

On the whole, my affairs have made quite good progress, in general, to this time but, from now on, for a while, I found life rather difficult. I was becoming a little impatient of the conditions I endured as Assistant Foreign Editor of the London Evening News, and wondered what kind of alterations I could make. I still found that most of the other members of the staff regarded me, and Foreign Affairs generally, as a strange activity which had nothing to do with them. It was obvious, too, that the readers of the paper, for the most part, ignored any foreign news. The Sub-Editors, Printers, and others took the same attitude by printing foreign news in a slightly careless way on occasions. Most of the copy came from Reuter's and other Agencies, and the few headed 'Evening News Correspondent', together with any other material produced by the Foreign Department, hardly seemed to fit into the paper. I do not suppose that we were able to attract many new readers, either.

Wondering what to do in this situation, I finally decided that my best step would be to apply for a position as Sub-Editor. I approached Mr Schofield, the Editor, and explained my wish to be a 'Sub'. He seemed a little doubtful about it, and said that the 'Subs' on the Evening Paper had to work very fast and start work very early. However, I persisted in my request, and he said he would bear it in mind.

After a few weeks, I was told to go to see Reg Willis, the Chief 'Sub'. I had always found him a pleasant fellow, certainly preferable to the 'higher-ups' in the Home News Department. We got on well enough and he said that if I wished to be a 'sub', I had better come and sit at the big table with the others.

I sat at the big table, surrounded by waste paper baskets and copy boys, who carried out news copy and brought in rather dirty mugs of tea. The mysteries of headline writing were explained, and I was told the name of each style of headline. Finally, I was allowed to sub-edit and write a headline for a few small items.

After I had progressed from 'NIBS' (NIBS from News in Brief — the smallest items) to copy with bigger headlines, I was told that, next week, I was to be the 'Early Sub'. The regular Early Sub, Conrad Davies, a tubby, comical Welshman and the humourist of the table, seemed to be pleased to get relief from this task. I was told to appear at the Office at 6.30 a.m. and that I would have to have a paper completed and sub-edited for the arrival of the Chief Sub at 8 o'clock.

At first, I think, Conrad came in fairly early to help me with my task but, before long, I found myself arriving at 6.30 a.m. (except on the days when I was a bit late) and having to gather all the copy together and make a complete paper out of it to lay in the Chief Sub's place at the head of the table before his arrival. My attempts were reasonably good but, on the whole, I found it difficult to produce headlines and edit the copy to high standards in the very short time available.

After a month or two of sub-editing, I regret to say I was called to see the Editor who told me that he did not think I was quick enough to be a Sub with the Evening News. In fact, I had a month's notice after being six years with the paper.

The next few months, I must say, I did not enjoy at the time but, looking back at a much later date in time, I suppose I can say that they were of some value. As I mentioned previously, my mother had served as a Nurse, and then became a Red Cross Commandant. From this, she acquired what could almost be called a fixation on medical matters. She tended to think that looking after your health was more important than anything else, and that Doctors were people to whom respect was to be given to a greater extent than she would ever give to anyone else.

From the idea that my mother had about medicine that medical men should be given priority over everyday matters, it was only a small step to the view that her knowledge of medicine and medical people entitled her to take charge of her surroundings and her family, the latter of whom happened to be all of the opposite sex. At times, she would consider herself superior to my father, although she admitted that he had succeeded academically, whereas she had been one of the naughty girls in the class at her girls' boarding school.

She wrote an imposing hand, and indeed, came from a very clever family (her father made a fortune in shipping and her brother became a Judge of the Court of Session), but she would say that she regretted that she had never worked hard at school.

After leaving the Evening News, I found myself more or less unemployed in London. As I had some private income, and the cost of living in London was not as great as now, I was not faced with the immediate problem of finding money or a job. I made friends with a small-time Travel Agent whom I met at the International Journalists' Club which was next door to his Agency near Piccadilly. He had a good position, but his Office was on the second or third floor. Eventually, I loaned him £500 and, for a time, he said I could come to help him with his work. I may say he later repaid my loan — with interest — and his business prospered exceedingly.

Eventually, my parents discovered that I was no longer working with the Evening News. I did not tell them much about what I was doing. My mother came to London, and installed herself at the Lansdowne Club, a sort of smart people's club which had opened in London, and eventually became the headquarters of the British Squash Championships.

It was not long before my mother was suggesting that I should see a Doctor, and a certain Lady Frankau was her favourite at the time. She was a Psychiatrist and well qualified to be a friend of my mother.

As I was not particularly busy myself, I thought it might be interesting to see what a psychiatrist had to say, so I did as my mother suggested. I have no doubt that Lady Frankau supplied my mother with a long report with suggestions that I should see other doctors and possibly agree to treatment.

The sort of existence that this led to went on for some months, but eventually I decided the existence was no longer of interest to me. I answered an advertisement calling for Representatives to sell Office equipment all over Britain, or rather England, and was accepted for interview at the Head Office of Sumlock Automaticket Limited. There I met the General Manager, Mr Nation-Tellery, who had a rather luxurious office in the West End of London.

It appears that I was accepted for the post and I was told to report for a Training Course of about ten days. I remember telling my mother about this, and she said that I should do no such thing. In fact, we parted company in the middle of Berkeley Square — I walked off on the path that was leading to Mr Nation-Tellery, and my mother retreated to the Lansdowne Club.

When I reported for the Course on the subject of 'Office Equipment and How to Sell It', I found myself one of a group of about twenty people, all men and mostly fairly young. We were told we were not expected to work the equipment, and were introduced to a girl demonstrator who operated large adding and calculating machines with unbelievable speed and skill. We heard about the history of the machines, the principles behind them and the territories into which England was divided for the purpose of selling them. I was told that the Scottish Office, which I was not particularly keen to go to anyway, was fully staffed.

At the end of the Course, we were asked to give our first and second choices of the area in which we would like to work, which meant having as a centre one of a number of English provincial towns. I had never visited Bristol — in fact, I have still not done so — and I thought that Bristol might be a pleasant place and the centre of an interesting stretch of country. I also decided that Leeds was half way between London and my home in Ayrshire and the principal stop on the trains which, at that time, went from London to Glasgow via Leeds and Kilmarnock. I remember that one of the would-be salesmen asked us all not to choose Southampton as it only had one vacancy and his elderly widowed mother lived there.

To my surprise, we were told by Mr Nation-Tellery that Bristol was the first choice of every single candidate except for the gentleman who preferred Southampton. We were called in individually to see the great man, and, when my turn came, he looked at me rather doubtfully and said "Do you really want to go to Leeds?" I replied that to me it was half-way home, and I thought I would be able to sell office equipment around such an important centre. "Well, every-one says Yorkshire folk are difficult to sell to," he said, "but once they get to know you, you are a friend for life."

On leaving the great man's presence, I found from the other candidates that none of them had the least wish to go to Leeds, and some showed surprise that I was ready to go there. I was rather shaken by all this, but decided there was really no way to get out of Leeds and try somewhere else.

I made my way up to Leeds, and called at the office of Sumlock Ltd., near the City centre. My instructions were to ask for the Branch Manager, Mr Richardson, and I found him quite a pleasant gentleman with a small RAF-type moustache. I rather got the impression that he had seen service with the Royal Air Force in the recent war. On Mr Richardson's instructions, I installed myself at The Mount Hotel. It was very much in a red brick area, near Leeds University. I think I stayed there about ten days, and still have a coat hanger inscribed with 'The Mount Hotel, Leeds' to remind me of being there.

My newly-arrived fellow representative working from the Leeds Office was a Canadian rather older than me. I was thirty-two, myself. He had a rather drawling way of speaking and seemed to have been in the commercial world so long that any energy for doing the job had long departed. He invited me for long sessions in Lyons tea shop in Leeds, where we whiled away hours at the firm's expense, discussing and doing nothing in particular. Luckily, I decided it would be best for me to drag myself away from him. I discovered in the end that he never made more than a very few convenient calls to seek business and, a month or so later, he parted company with our employers.

Mr Richardson showed me a map of the West Riding, divided into coloured sections, and informed me that I had been allotted an area including Huddersfield and Halifax, stretching nearly up to Wakefield. It was a heavily industrialised and populated area, not far from Leeds, and I think it was something of a compliment to me to have been given it. I was also introduced to my demonstrator — a very smart young lady indeed, who was to accompany me and demonstrate the machines when I had aroused interest in a customer. She was beautifully made up and well dressed. Her nails, in particular, were most impressive — fairly colourful and not too long. I can think of many amusing incidents connected with my calls around the businesses and factories of the West Riding. Once, at a place called Ossett (which, like Pudsey, is something of a joke to Yorkshiremen), I called at a firm called Wilbey & Buckley. I went brightly in and asked to speak to Mr Wilbey. "Mr Wilbey's busy, lad" said the gentleman I was addressing, giving me a rather unfriendly look. I replied chirpily "Then I'll speak to Mr Buckley." "That tha woant, lad" said the gentleman, who evidently was Mr Buckley, "If tha doant leave soon, I'll kick thee downstairs," so I made a rapid exit. My liking for Ossett was not increased after this and there is, indeed a Yorkshire saying "I'll go to Ossett," which is used to express surprise, when something unlikely occurs.

Another time, I called at what seemed to be quite a large firm, somewhere in the neighbourhood of Huddersfield. I knew the name of the managing director, so I spoke to a small, scruffy old gentleman in a dirty khaki overall who was sitting on a kind of stool in the corner. "I would like to see Mr so and so," I said to him. "What dost tha want, lad?, I'm him," he replied, which I found rather disconcerting. I brought out some sales talk, but I did not think I made much progress.

In my moments off work, I prospected around in the neighbourhood of The Mount Hotel, to find somewhere I could stay on a more permanent basis. I think Mr Richardson had already hinted that I could not stay more than two weeks at The Mount at the firm's expense.

This period marks my first acquaintance with Leeds University. It seemed to consist of a very large central white concrete building, embellished with a few statues, and surrounded by rather mean streets of red brick houses, many of which were embellished with inscriptions like "Department of Geography," "Department of Wool Technology," "Department of Psychology" and so on. In one of the streets, I called on a couple who seemed to make a living by letting rooms and providing meals.

The couple were a Durham husband with a wife who came from Leicestershire. She was rather glamorous, but he did not impress me particularly. He seemed to be the kind that took a pride on speaking in a rough dialect, whereas she, although speaking in a Leicestershire dialect, tried to make it sound more refined. They agreed that I could take a room there, and breakfast and evening meal would be provided.

There seemed to be one other permanent resident, a very smart and pleasant young man who was a supervisor in some factory — a clothing factory, I think.

I began to wonder if the landlady selected her tenants because they were young men who interested her. She was usually ready to carry on a flirtatious conversation with the other young man, and I wondered whether I could get her to take an interest in me.

After a few months, my efforts were successful. Whereas the flirtation between the lady and the other young man (a year or two younger than me) was just casual and superficial, I began to think she was transferring her affections to me in a more serious way. I did my best to converse with her rather bony husband in a cheerful way, and he certainly had no objection. He seemed quite pleased that his wife was happy in our company.

The relationship between me and the landlady developed in a way which, looking back on it, might appear quite normal. But, at the time, it was something which I found very novel (actually not quite novel!) and exciting. She told me, after a while, that she was unable to have children, so there was no reason for us to control our relationship in any way. In fact, she was not really a happy person, and I have no doubt that her inability to have children contributed to this. Her husband, rather older than herself, and a thin, bony, hard-bitten Northcountryman, was not a person to cope with her warm, feminine and passionate nature, so I may as well admit that, for several months, at least, my relationship with this lady proceeded in a very intimate fashion.

My efforts at selling office equipment around the West Riding of Yorkshire continued. I made a fair number of sales, though not all that many, and began calling mainly on the bigger and more important firms in the area. There was a motor car and tractor manufacturer, David Brown Ltd., of whom I met the Managing Director, who gave me a long talk on his plans for motor racing, although he did not order any equipment! I also met the Managing Director of a large chemical company, and the head of the Accounts Department of a textile manufacturer who had recently opened a branch in Northern Ireland. I think I nearly made a sale there, and I was impressed by the prosperity and expansion of the firm. I told my father that this was a prosperous firm and he said he would invest some money in its shares. Several years later, he said he wished he had invested in the textile firm I recommended, as the shares had done so well. After a few months careering round West Yorkshire by train, by bus and in a secondhand car which I bought, I was told by Mr Richardson that he did not think I was a person who had a long-term prosperous future as a machinery salesman. I may say that the Canadian who spent his time in Lyons Corner House Café had left long before this.

As my notice was expiring, I went to the Labour Exchange in Leeds, and sold my personality and talents to such an effect that I was invited to join the Youth Employment Service of the West Riding County Council. I was told to report to County Headquarters at Wakefield to be interviewed by the Head of the Department. I did this and was accepted, being told to report to the Wakefield office of the Youth Employment Service to gain training and experience.

About this time too I did an evening course in Philosophy which was provided by the Professor of Philosophy at Leeds University, who was highly regarded in his field.

I found the personnel of the Youth Employment Service at Wakefield — which included the staff running the whole West Riding as well as those running the Wakefield Office — quite an interesting and pleasant crowd. I was one of the juniors there, and I think I started off by helping the girls with the filing. I was astonished to find that there were files about very many of the young people of the area with all kinds of intimate details and reports provided by their school headmasters and others. It made me wonder what details about me had been circulated from one end of Britain to the other in the course of my various activities.

I spent a few months at the Youth Employment Headquarters at Wakefield, which I found both interesting and enjoyable. For a time, I was perhaps rather jealous of a fairly tall, very smart young man who seemed to be the centre of every-one's attention. Like me, although a little younger, he seemed to be a junior in the office who was learning about the job of Youth Employment Officer. His appearance was, perhaps, impressive but his conversational powers seemed to me to be ordinary. "Who's that young man, over there?" I asked one of the girls, not long after I had arrived. "Don't you know? That is David Prince, the son of Councillor Prince who comes from Wakefield, and is on many of the County Council's most important Committees," I was told.

"The way things are, I am sure he will be a Youth Employment Officer in no time at all." I cannot say that this made me like the young Mr Prince any the more, but I could not deny that he was a pleasant young man, who seemed to have a way with the ladies, and even the men.

After a time, so far as a I can remember, David Prince left the office to be Assistant Youth Employment Officer somewhere in the County. I, too, was eventually called into see the Head of Department, who asked me if I had ever met Miss Freeman-Archer. I said I had not, so he told me that she was Youth Employment Officer in the Harrogate Office. I might find her a surprising person, but if I wished, I could go as her Assistant to Harrogate.

I agreed to the proposition without really enquiring whether I was to be Assistant Youth Employment Officer or Youth Employment Officer's Assistant. Indeed, this question was never quite resolved — just as it had never been resolved in London whether I was Assistant Foreign Editor or Foreign Editor's Assistant. As far as I can remember, my pay was more that of a Youth Employment Officer's Assistant, but the point was never pressed, and I was certainly free to call myself at times Assistant Youth Employment Officer.

I duly made my way to Harrogate and met Miss Freeman-Archer. She was a spinster of uncertain age, and soon told me that she had been brought up as a member of the "ascendancy" in Southern Ireland. "What great times we used to have, riding with the So and So Hounds," she told me. "What a lot of things you could do in Ireland that would cost far too much in England." I endeavoured to make the right kind of remark in reply to her observations, and tried to get on with the dog, who seemed to be her permanent companion in the office. As far as I can remember, I got on all right in Harrogate, and was eventually called back to see the boss in Wakefield. "How did you get on with Miss Freeman-Archer?" he said to me. "All right," I answered, and I think I detected a look of surprise on his face when I said that. "There is a vacancy at present at Hemsworth," he continued, "could you report there next Monday and meet the Officer there?"

Making enquiries and consulting a map, I found that Hemsworth was quite a long way from Leeds, near Doncaster, and had a railway station. I duly arrived there by train and met the solitary gentleman who was holding the fort for the West Riding County Council.

While my official career was taking this new and, to me, unexpected turn, my private life was not without interest. My friendship with the lady in Mount Preston in the red brick area near Leeds University, continued. I also joined the English-Speaking Union and became fairly active in the Younger Members' Group.

The English-Speaking Union in Leeds was a body which held monthly luncheons in a hotel near the town centre, at which a speaker gave a talk. I attended some of these, but discovered that they were more popular with the older members than with the Young Members' Group. The latter had their own functions, which consisted of meeting together or of going away on various excursions, some connected with sport and some not.

The E.S.U. Younger Members seemed to be something of a socially superior set. They did not speak with Yorkshire accents and many of them had parents who were prominent in various businesses. I even met the son of a Leeds City Alderman who, with his wife, gave garden parties and was prominent both with the Council and as a Conservative. Their son, however, seemed to be giving them some worry as his main interest in life was being a member of a jazz band which provided music at many functions that the young man's father would certainly not attend.

On the whole, there were more girls than boys in the Younger Members' Group, which I must admit was the way I wanted things. I had always felt, in Ayrshire, that where-ever one went there were about two girls to every three boys, which made it difficult for me to be as friendly as I wished with the other sex. In the E.S.U. Younger Members, I found myself making new friends, both boys and girls, but rather more of the latter.

One girl I met, who seemed to me rather attractive, was apparently Supervisor of the Non-Nursing Staff at Leeds Infirmary. Her parents lived at Burley-in-Wharfdale, and I found, in time, that her father was a Director of an old family firm which consisted of the most expensive large department store in Bradford. Her mother too came from a successful business family.

It appeared that this girl, whose name was April,

organised the Domestic Staff at Leeds Infirmary with great efficiency. She also liked to have a regular boyfriend, and apparently they had been an interesting and remarkable collection of men. The present one was a high-up Police Inspector, and he and April used to go for long walks, and vanish for long periods in the Inspector's car.

However, I found myself getting on fairly well with April, and was invited to join a party at dinner at home, followed by a dance at Ilkley. I asked her to tell me the way to get to her home, which she did. I had not been to Burley-in-Wharfdale at all, and would have been wiser to have reconnoitred the address prior to the evening of the dinner. As it was, I had allowed too little time, was mis-directed at Burley and eventually arrived at the dinner, in my dinner dress, as it was nearing its last course. However, every-one said I was not to worry, and we went to the dance which, in fact, I enjoyed.

April and I became friendly, and I asked her if she would like to go out with me. I did not quite trust my secondhand car, and worked out a train journey on the Leeds to Edinburgh train as far as Melrose, where we were to get out of the train and shortly afterwards take another one back to Leeds. The return would be rather late at night, but as April had her own flat in Leeds, we agreed that the time of return did not matter.

Remarkably enough, we set off on this journey to Melrose in winter, as I remember; the train was warm and we reached Melrose at a late hour. On the return journey we had the compartment to ourselves and, as has been observed before, there are many advantages to a couple in having a train compartment to themselves. I certainly was friendly with the young lady, without taking it to the ultimate conclusion.

Sometime, when I had been talking to April, the point had been raised by one of us that she might like to come to see me at my residence at Mount Preston. This was agreed on, but it had not occurred to me before that time that there were times when it was not good, from a man's point of view, for two ladies to meet each other. When April arrived at Mount Preston, my landlady was there and "if looks could kill" April would certainly have emerged in bad health.

This meeting of the two ladies was most unfortunate for me. April said that she would not come again to see me at Mount Preston and, altogether, seemed to want to keep me at a distance. I did not like the idea of my life at Mount Preston continuing indefinitely in its present way, so I decided to look for other accommodation.

Meanwhile, I was still carrying on with my work on behalf of the West Riding Youth Employment Service. I went to meet the Officer at the Hemsworth office, which I reached after a fairly long journey by train from Leeds. The first thing to be seen on leaving the train was an enormous coal mine spoil heap beside which was all the equipment of a very large coal mine. As I left the station, I was able to see the rest of Hemsworth which seemed to consist only of some rows of cottages and a public house. I found the Youth Employment Office which, so far as I can remember, was rather small. I met the gentleman who was running it, who told me he was going abroad for three weeks holiday, and that I would be taking charge of the office until he came back. He said there was not a great deal of work. "What can you say to the young people who come in?" he said. "For the boys it is mostly work in the coal mine that you can offer, and for the girls, really nothing at all, unless you give them particulars from one of the other offices." We sat down in chairs and began to talk and, in the course of a day or two, I was able to find out a few things about him. He was a native of Tees-side and had worked for Imperial Chemical Industries, there. "At that time, there would be a row of men sitting at a row of instruments, whereas, later, they put all the instruments together and one man did the lot. Do you know how they used to stop one of us falling asleep on the job? We sat on a chair with one leg and, if you went to sleep, you fell over and woke up."

At about 12 o'clock, I asked him what I should do about lunch. He told me he brought his with him and, if I had not brought mine, I could go to the public house, where they would serve me a cooked lunch, I did this, and found that they had cooked the lunch rather earlier in the day. It was now cold and I did not enjoy trying to eat cold roast beef in cold gravy with cold vegetables. I decided not to try that sort of lunch again.

The gentleman in question duly went on his holiday abroad, and I held the fort at Hemsworth until his return. As he said, there was not very much to do, as people did not come into the Office often. When they did, as often as not it seemed to me the best thing to do was refer them to the Wakefield Office, which they could contact by telephone or in person. I suppose I explained to one or two of the young men how they could go round and see the colliery officials, giving them the "magical" green card. I think I got my landlady in Leeds to supply me with sandwiches for lunch, and my period at Hemsworth passed rather slowly until it came to an end.

I am not sure whether I went back to the Harrogate Office but, about this time, I was told that I was to go and assist the Youth Employment Officer at Skipton. I remember the lady in the Wakefield Office saying with bated breath, as it were, "Do you know that Mr X is a Communist?" "Is he really?" I answered, and wondered what a Communist Youth Employment Officer looked like. Perhaps I visualised someone in a cloth cap with hunched shoulders and a rather dirty jacket.

When I reached Skipton, I was full of interest to see what the gentleman looked like. I was disappointed to see that he looked like everybody else, and was even wearing quite a smart suit. I looked carefully to see if he was wearing a red tie, but he was not. He never spoke to me on the subject of Communism, but I seemed to remember getting the impression that he was on the Labour side of politics. This may be enough for some of the more Conservative ladies in the Wakefield Office to describe him as a Communist.

I settled down into the usual Youth Employment work at Skipton. There was also a lady in the office whom I found rather pleasant, if motherly, who came from a small village outside Skipton, Embsay, where she lived all her life. She told me the Skipton Office also ran the Sedbergh Office. I knew Sedbergh, one of the furthest possible northwest points in Yorkshire, a very long way indeed from the County Buildings in Wakefield. Even to get to Sedbergh from Skipton entailed catching a bus at about half past seven in the morning to open the office in time. This was done, I think, two days a week. The lady said to me reassuringly, that she did not think I would have to go to Sedbergh, as she had been doing it almost single handed, I gather, for a good many years.

The Youth Employment Officer and I never became very friendly, and our conversation was mainly confined to official matters. Perhaps he regarded me as an aristocrat who ought to be liquidated, though he certainly did not say so. He did not talk very much, and what he said did not show any strong views. The lady, on the other hand, talked a lot, and I was able to find out what life had been like in a fairly remote Yorkshire Dales village in the last few years.

Towards the end of 1954, I had the same kind of message from the Youth Employment Service as had reached me on previous occasions. They did not think I was the sort of person they would want to employ on a permanent basis and gave me notice to look for other activities, from a certain date. Nothing daunted, I decided that there was a strong demand for teachers throughout the country. I knew there were several teacher training units in Leeds and district. As a Graduate, however, I would qualify for a one-year Teacher Training Course at the Leeds University Institute of Education, which would give me, at the end, a Graduate Certificate of Education. With this, I would be able to teach in almost any State school, and, no doubt, would be regarded as unusually well qualified for any teaching post for which I might apply in the Private education sector. In the sudden feeling of optimism about teaching which came over me, I saw myself in the future as a teacher in a State school, or possibly as the owner of some kind of Private School of which I had experienced quite a number at earlier stages of my life.

No doubt I rather conveniently persuaded myself to forget the time when I had taught for a while at a "Private Preparatory" School at Oxford. I had not really had the right manner there for keeping order in class, and had not really enjoyed the experience of teaching, although I thought I knew enough to teach several subjects. I believed, too, that I had a liking for children, and the ability to get on well with them. I forgot that, though this might be true with small numbers of children of mixed sex, when it comes to teaching a large classroom full of badly behaved small boys, I had not been happy or successful.

Putting all cares aside, I duly applied to Leeds University Institute of Education to join their one-year Graduate Course. They seemed pleased to see me, as I supposed Oxford University Graduates were fairly uncommon in Leeds. The Deputy Head of the Institute was a Scot, and I was able to lure him into talking about his part of Scotland while I talked about mine. I filled in the appropriate forms and before long was told that I had been accepted for the Graduate Education Course.

When the time came, I made a good start at Leeds University. I was given a list of books, which I read, and soon began to adopt my own educational theories. I believed that men, or rather children, are naturally good and that if they were treated, or rather taught the right way, they would naturally want to learn, and difficulties would be small and negligible. Soon I got to know many of the other students, and was able and willing to argue educational theories with them as desired. I later wrote some essays which went down well with our lecturers. I enjoyed the lectures, and was always willing to give my views in class or out of it.

Gradually, the members of the post-graduate Certificate of Education Course came to know each other. It was the custom to meet for coffee-breaks at every possible opportunity in the refectory, which was a kind of self-service canteen, where people sat around tables. I became one of a group of four or five people who generally got together, with additions or subtractions of other students from time to time.

I remember there was a student called Peter, rather small and talkative, whose home I think was in Cumbria's Lake District. There was a girl called Anne, medium-sized and plump, who came from Harrogate. It was amusing to see both of them trying to make friends with each other, and sometimes succeeding. One felt that each could sense the other's limitations, but decided to be friends with the other because they would possibly never get better opportunities.

I also took part in out-of-college activities. I joined the Leeds University Youth Hostel Association, when I heard that they were going for what sounded a very pleasant weekend in Derbyshire. We took train or bus to Sheffield, then by bus out to Edale, where a brand new youth hostel had just been built. We walked the hills and dales of Derbyshire and in the evening arrived at the hostel. Dinner was unexciting, consisting I think of eggs, chips and baked beans. Eventually we repaired to the dormitories, one for each sex (unlike French hostels where they are said to be mixed). I remember spending the night with one prickly sheet and one even pricklier blanket.

Next morning after breakfast the Warden appeared and gave us each a task to do. I was given a mop and a wringing bucket filled with water. I had never mopped a floor in my life, so proceeded to spill the water on the floor and tried to mop it up with the mop. The Warden appeared and said "Are you trying to play a joke?" I answered by asking him for advice on how to mop. He refused to take me seriously and told me that I had better leave the building. I said "I am thinking of joining the Youth Hostel Association, how much is the subscription?"

He did not answer. My friends eventually joined me outside and we made our way home via Sheffield, a remarkably quiet place on Sunday. I never went out again with the Leeds University Y.H.A., nor did I ever join the Youth Hostel Association.

I made friends with a post graduate student of the University, who had obtained a science degree some five years before. He did a little research in the Laboratories, and in return had to do every-body's dirty and unpleasant jobs which they wished to avoid. He had a tiny salary of two or three pounds a week and wanted to marry, but could not. His hobby, it appeared, was athletics and he was a member of the University Team.

I told my friend, who we will call Charles, that I had once been a long-distance runner. "Can you do the 440 yards?" he said. "Yes," I answered. "Good," he replied. "We need someone to run against Manchester University on Saturday week."

I was rather horrified at this, as I had never been good at the 440 yards or anything less than about six miles. However, I found out where the University Athletic grounds were (outside a women's hostel, I was told to encourage me) so I duly went there and ran round and round the track, 440 yards at a time. I had rather hoped that the girls would come out of the hostel to watch me, but they did not.

After a few days' practice, the great day of the Athletic Meeting against Manchester arrived. We all piled into a bus, drove across the Pennines and reached Manchester. It was very obvious that Manchester was a very much larger University than Leeds, and had a very much better athletic team. I had managed to borrow a pair of spiked shoes that fitted me but nevertheless regret to say that I came in last. After the meeting we went to the Students' Union where much friendly rivalry between Manchester and Leeds showed itself and ate baked beans on toast, after playing table tennis.

I remained friendly with Charles, but his disgust at his working conditions and low pay continued. One day he told me that he had obtained a post as an Agricultural and Scientific adviser in Bolivia, he thought somewhere near Lake Titicaca. I had a chance to display my wide general knowledge, "Isn't that where there are frogs with only two legs, or perhaps two legs very long and two very short?" I asked. He was not sure, but thought it might be so.

I was given my first period of Teaching Practice at a Secondary Modern School in Leeds. I remember going to school, meeting the Headmaster, and being introduced to the Staff Room. I was given a timetable of classes which allowed me a fair number of free periods. As far as I can remember, I taught English and French.

Everything I had read about over-large classes in British State Schools proved to be true. The problems of coping with some forty boys and girls who had no real ambition to learn anything in class were formidable. Making fun of the teacher was a popular occupation. One method was to ask a seemingly innocent question and then laugh uproariously at the answer.

I struggled on through this first period of teaching practice, knowing that it was bound to end in a week or two. The other staff, including the Headmaster, were not much interested in my classes, being no doubt too busy with their own. There was one young lady in the Staff Room who seemed to take a lot of trouble with her appearance and make-up; in fact she was quite good-looking. When she was not there one of the men on the staff told me that she could create problems, as he said she was always on the look-out for boyfriends of almost any age.

I thought I might as well try my hand after this. I managed to get into a conversation with her in private, and asked her if she would come out for an evening with me in Leeds. To my surprise, she took great offence. "If you want to go out with me, surely you know you should ask my parents first," she said. I said I didn't know but I would try what she wanted. However, I could not imagine how I could get to know her parents, or even their address, so I suppose this became one of my less successful relationships. I remember reading the notice of her engagement a year or two later in the Yorkshire Post.

After some three or four weeks the struggle of teaching practice came to an end, and I was glad to return to what for me was the comparatively easy life of lectures and essays. There was one rather good-looking lady lecturer, but I was warned it was no use trying to talk to her as she did not like men and in fact preferred lady friends. The men lecturers varied from the ancient to the formidable to the pathetic, including one who was desperately anxious that every member of his class should buy a new copy of a text book on education that he had written.

There was one student in the group who it was said gave all the girls "a funny feeling inside," and indeed the men students did not find him likeable either. One girl said to me that there had been an argument among some of the girls as to whether they liked me or not; apparently there were a number who approved of me and a number who equally strongly did not.

One day there appeared on the notice board in the Leeds University Main Building an advertisement for a dance which apparently was to be given by something called Ghost Hall. Like other dances it was to take place in the Students' Union, but the Union was to be converted for the occasion into the abode of ghosts. "Prepare To Meet Your Doom," said the advertisement "And Come To Meet the Ghosts, Goblins and Witches of Ghost Hall." I made some enquiries about this dance. It appeared that Ghost Hall did not exist, but was alleged to be the Hall of Residence of Leeds University Students who actually lived at home, in places easily reached from the University. I decided I would go to this dance, if only to meet some of the students who were actually Yorkshire folk living in the Leeds district.

I rather think that all who came to this dance were supposed to dress up as ghosts, witches, hobgoblins, etc. However, with my usual laziness and dislike of changing clothes, I did not do so. I arrived at the dance with some of my friends and was impressed by the eerie decorations of the room which were mainly in shades of black and lurid yellow. Suitably ghostly music was no doubt being produced by a darkly clad orchestra.

I remember looking at one girl who I think was dressed mainly in yellow as a rather pleasant-looking witch. I looked at her and somebody said "Don't you know her? That's Norma, she's quite a character. Would you like to meet her?" I agreed, was introduced to Norma, and I think asked her to dance. She seemed to approve of me and I found her interesting. She had a pleasant well-educated voice. Her parents it seemed stayed at a place called Castleford, but she did not seem like a Castleford girl. She told me she had an Upper Second degree in Classics at London University, and was in fact doing the same graduate certificate of education course that I was. No doubt after the lectures she immediately went home to her parents in Castleford, which was probably why I had not met her up to then.

56

Norma was a rather slender girl with blonde hair. I think we arranged to meet next day or at any rate soon after the dance. We became very friendly and after a time she asked if I would like to meet her parents. Naturally I said yes, and this was arranged. I took my rather inferior second-hand car out to Castleford, to a private housing estate called Barnsdale. Outside Norma's parents' house (the family name was Harris) was a street lamp and in parking I knocked it over with my car. Norma came out of the house and told me not to worry. I went in and met her father, who apparently managed a large bakery, and her mother, whom I thought a good-looking if slightly domineering woman.

I continued my studies at the University and saw a fair amount of Norma. She said that a van from the Council had arrived and repaired the damage to the street lamp, without making enquiries as to how it was caused.

I continued to find the theoretical side of education interesting, and had no trouble keeping up with studies as well as taking part in leisure activities. After a while we were given details of our final period of Teaching Practice. I was to go to a privately owned boys' boarding school called Woodhouse Grove, a few miles out of Leeds beside the main railway line to the North.

My teaching practice at Woodhouse Grove turned out for the most part to be a series of disasters. I was instructed to make an appointment with the Headmaster, the Rev Mr Pritchard, and arranged to see him about 3 p.m. I decided to take the train to Apperley Bridge Station, very close to the school, but found there wasn't a suitable train. So I travelled to the next station beyond Apperley Bridge which was Shipley, and on arrival found I had gone several miles too far. I had counted on taking a taxi, but there was none at the station and I had a long walk to the town centre and beyond before I found one. When eventually I was shown into Mr Pritchard's study it was well past the time appointed and he clearly was not over-pleased to see me. However, he talked a bit about the school, showed me the staffroom and gave me a time-table.

The next day I arrived at the school in good time and tried to find my way around it. It was next to the main line from Leeds to Carlisle and the wall surrounding the school yard had been specially provided with low places so that boys who wished could stand and look at passing trains.

The school had been founded by and for Methodists during the 19th century. The heavy stone buildings had a solid, Victorian, Yorkshire look about them. In the school and the classrooms were open fires. Frequently I encountered members of a corps of uncouth, illiterate, hard-bitten Yorkshiremen whose main duty appeared to be carrying buckets of coal around to heat the school. Even the boys seemed to have a hard, unbending Yorkshire look and many of them seemed to be no more intelligent than the carriers of the coal.

Eventually I found myself faced with a class of the boys of Woodhouse Grove, from the lower end of the school both in age and scholastic attainments. I found on the whole that I had to shout to get them to listen to me and about once in every teaching period a diversion was caused by a Yorkshire tyke arriving with a coal bucket. Trying to teach French I found particularly difficult; somehow fast smooth-flowing Parisian French seemed particularly foreign to these slow speaking, insular Yorkshire lads.

Whereas in the Leeds Secondary Modern School classroom disturbances were regarded as normal, with no one paying much attention, disturbances in my new fee-paying school were immediately noticed by other members of the staff. During free periods spent in the staffroom, of which I had a fair number, I was liable to hear complaints about my classes from other staff members. No doubt they were passed on to the Headmaster, and when an inspector came from the Leeds University Institute of Education, no doubt he heard them too.

I became an accepted figure in the staff room, helping people do their crossword puzzles and occasionally going out to buy cigarettes and other small items from the local sweet shop. I tried to make my lessons interesting to the boys, with somewhat limited success. Occasionally I helped with sporting activities, even refereeing a game of Rugby football although I have never been a keen Rugby man.

After a few weeks spent in this fashion I was summoned to the Institute of Education at Leeds, to be told that I had failed my teaching practise. This was bad news, but I must confess I felt rather relieved that I was not to spend the next few years of my life in a lively classroom.

By now I had changed my place of residence, moving first of all to lodgings found for me by the University at Headingley, and then to a large room in another part of

Headingley which I found for myself. It appeared that Headingley, with its cricket ground where test matches were played, considered itself superior to the rest of Leeds.

I remained friendly with Norma, a girl who was studying Education with me and whose home was at Castleford. She told me one of the reasons she had so quickly become interested in me. "I looked you up in the reference book in the library and found you were the son of a Baronet." Apparently no other girl I had ever met had done this and perhaps if I had told them about my family it would have aroused their interest. Luckily Norma did not know about Evelyn, but she found out about April when I took her to a meeting of the English-Speaking Union Younger Members' Group. She must have heard quite a lot, because for many years to come I would be reproached that I did not love her and that I really preferred April to Norma. Possibly she had an inferiority complex, refusing to believe it when I told her that I found her as interesting and attractive a person as I had met.

I continued to read a great deal. One day I noticed an advertisement in the Yorkshire Evening Post, "Partner Wanted for Textile Factory in Bradford." I answered this and was given the address of a man who turned out to be an Irish-born sewing machine mechanic. Not a particularly impressive figure, he told me that he and a tailor in Leeds of Jewish origin named Brostoff had taken the lease of a small clothing factory, fitted it with sewing machines and proposed to engage machinists to make ladies' overalls and similar garments. Work had never really started at the factory, Mr Brostoff was losing interest, and would I like to come in with them and get the place going?

As things were, I seemed to be in a position to try and do something for this enterprise. Not much money was required, or so it seemed and with my partner's help it should be possible to make good progress. In fact I soon found out that he was not my partner, for he had invested no money in the enterprise. I bought some cloth, my partner offered to cut it according to patterns and two or three girls were engaged to sew the garments together.

Soon I began to see through the motives of my so-called partner more clearly. We had engaged two or three part-timers for a day shift, and he proposed to engage more for an evening shift of which he would take charge. I asked why he wanted to start an evening shift and eventually found out that he thought he would have a free hand with the girl or girls in the evening while I was away.

I was still living in Leeds, which is some ten miles from Bradford but very much a different world. It seemed to be very rare for anyone to have interests in both cities; in fact I never found anyone apart from myself who did have such interests. It appeared that no-one resided in Bradford who could possibly manage to live elsewhere. Leeds on the other hand was a place where the inhabitants varied from the very poor to the very rich and cultivated, including a large Jewish population. Culture in Bradford was definitely at a lower level, although many large fortunes had been made there. "Where there's muck there's money," said Bradford people, and as soon as they made some money they left the city.

I kept in touch with Norma, and was surprised to learn at the end of the academic year that she had failed her exam in Education. "It's your fault, it's because I'm in love with you," she told me. I was certainly impressed and pleased to find someone who apparently liked me even in my less successful moments.

From time to time I went home to visit the family, and sometimes my father would come to see me. My mother had died from a brain tumour a year or two before.

I thought I would invite Norma to come and stay at my father's house in Scotland, so I did this and she accepted. It appeared that she had a rather romantic outlook on life. She was friendly with one of her former school teachers, a lady from the Isle of Man, who told Norma Manx legends and fairy tales and even tried to teach her Manx. No doubt Norma thought Scotland to be just as romantic as Miss Killip had described the Isle of Man to her.

Norma certainly seemed to be impressed by my father's large mansion and the trees and farms surrounding it. My father was becoming friendly with a divorced lady living about a mile away, and whom he eventually married. I certainly was becoming rather tired of the solitary life and was glad that Norma seemed to be so fond of me. I let it be understood by her that we were to become engaged.

After a while we decided to make a formal announcement of the engagement. I arranged for the notice to appear in The Times, The Yorkshire Post and The Glasgow Herald.

The reactions to the announcement were fairly considerable. Norma by this time had left the Leeds University Department of Education, and was in fact working as a sales girl in Lewis's department store stationery department. When the local papers saw from the engagement notice that she was to marry the son of a Scottish Baronet, reporters telephoned her home and then the store where she worked. A reporter and photographer came to see her. Soon the headline spread across the Yorkshire Evening News "Leeds Shop Girl To Wed Baronet's Son." Several people came up to me and said they did not know my father was a Baronet; I began to wish that I had told more people about it. I rather think that some Yorkshire girls and their mothers wished that they had paid me more attention.

Various business offers came through the post. A fashionable firm of photographers offered to take a studio photograph of Norma at what seemed to be a low price, provided they had the right to publish it. We accepted this offer and the photographer indeed turned out to be excellent. I am not sure how much it was published, but in any case that did not concern us a great deal.

I was still continuing to work at my factory in Bradford. I decided to tell the sewing machine mechanic who was supposed to be a partner that I no longer required his services and as he had no money invested in the enterprise there was nothing he could do about this. I advertised in the Bradford paper for a part-time cloth cutter, and received a few replies. I found someone who could cut the cloth satisfactorily from patterns, and indeed even make his own patterns. Eventually I learned enough about the art or skill of laying and cutting cloth to be able to do it myself. Sometimes I would buy in patterns from outside sources; I never became skilful enough to make my own patterns.

I kept in touch with Mr Brostoff, the Leeds tailor who had been one of the founders of the business. He told me he had no wish to travel the slightly over ten miles to Bradford to take part in its affairs. Eventually I offered him £100 to leave the business and hand it over to me, and he agreed to do this.

I read about a block of flats that was being built in the Leeds suburb of Headingley. They were to be attractive flats surrounded by a large garden and those who wished to live in them were to be offered the opportunity of buying a single flat outright. The idea of selling a single flat in a block was apparently at that time something of a novelty. The project (the flats were to be called Regency Court) was in the hands of an estate agent who did not seem to be well-known among the lawyers and estate agents of Leeds.

I thought I had better engage my own lawyer, so I called on a firm of solicitors who seemed to be located in the right business district of the city. I was shown into the office of one of the partners, Mr Michael Wilde, who seemed quite a likeable person. In fact we became good friends. He introduced me to his wife and family and I found that knowing him was of great value to me over a period of a good many years.

Norma and I got together to fit out the flat in Regency Court as soon as it was built. It was, in fact, not a flat but a "maisonette," consisting of a part of the top two floors of a three-storey block of flats. I bought it with the help of a mortgage; and no sooner had the concrete dried than we were fitting it out with carpets and furniture. I had a friend, Keith Batty, who was assistant manager at Maples store in Leeds. He was able to advise us about furnishing, and also obtain several attractive items of carpets and furniture for us at what seemed to be quite a low price.

With my love for foreign travel it seemed a good idea to me to arrange a honeymoon in France and Italy, and Norma agreed to this. I wrote to a hotel situated on a mountain above Lake Como, which was connected with the town of Como by a funicular railway. We were to fly to Milan, go by train to Como, and then to the hotel at Brunate above the Lake. A week there was to be followed by staying with friends who had a villa on the Italian Riviera a few miles from Genoa.

Finally the great day drew near. With some difficulty we had arranged where we were to be married. Neither of us were very keen for the ceremony to take place at Castleford, where my wife's parents lived, as it was some way from Leeds and would be difficult for guests to reach. I saw a Church of England vicar, who recommended Headingley as my residence, but I was not very keen on this. I asked if it was possible to arrange for a church in central Leeds to be made use of, and after first saying it was not possible he suggested Leeds Parish Church, as being a Leeds resident I would have the right to be married there. This suited both Norma and me, so we arranged this, booked a hotel in Boar Lane for the reception and made the usual arrangements about bridesmaids, best man, wedding stationery and the use of a choir. As far as the church was concerned, I thought the prices were low, and even the other expenses did not add up to a great amount.

Both Leeds Parish Church and the Boar Lane Hotel struck the guests as interesting old places with considerable life in them still, and the wedding was generally regarded as a success. Norma and I set off from Leeds city station, spending our first night at the Great Northern Hotel, King's Cross, London. Next day we flew to Milan, and by the evening had arrived at the town of Como, from which we took a funicular to Brunate above the lake. Both of us seemed to be enjoying the journey so far.

Norma had shown unexpected talent and enthusiasm which I did not know she possessed. She was rather surprised by the room given us by the superior hotel at Brunate, which included a bathroom separated from the bedroom mainly by a partition of glass. However, even this did not upset her for long; she was quite a different person from the rather shy and far from forward girl I had known before the wedding. It was, perhaps an indication of the difference that a wedding ring will often make in the behaviour of a woman.

We stayed a week at Brunate, taking the opportunity to travel up and down Lake Como in the fairly large boats which sail on it. There are some fine villas and gardens to be seen, beside the warm Italian alpine hills rising above the lake. One day we went by train to Milan (there was a local steam railway as well as the electrified State railway which was available for this journey). Our photograph was taken by a rather villainous looking photographer in a Carrozza, or horse-carriage.

The photographer gave me a ticket with which I could claim the photograph when it was ready. I gave him the money, and the address near Genoa where we were to be the following week. However, nothing arrived, and it was lucky that we had an introduction to a lady in Milan who was the director of an art gallery there devoted mainly to the works of Guardi. Sometime after returning to Britain I wrote to her enclosing the photographer's ticket, and eventually she was able to send us the photograph of us sitting behind the horse in the carrozza outside Milan Cathedral.

From Milan we went for a few days to Sori, on the coast near Genoa, where an English couple had set up a superior boarding house surrounded by a fine garden leading down to the rocky shore. A number of people were staying there, most of them elderly holiday-makers who seemed pleased to see a young couple in their midst. We enjoyed our time there, leaving on a train for Paris which provided a long day's journey through the Alps with all the comforts of a second-class carriage and refreshment car. We travelled with some people who seemed to have started their journey at Naples. For them it was a long journey, but for us the trip from Genoa to Paris was very pleasant. One night in Paris, and then we took the plane back to Leeds.

I am afraid life in Regency Court, Leeds, was something of an anti-climax after the visit to Italy and France. Regency Court, with its newly planted gardens, was pleasant enough, but we found our neighbours to be a mixed collection: some were pleasant enough, others were typically self-contained and aggressive Yorkshiremen. However, we managed to keep going, and settle down into a kind of routine.

Every working day I went to Bradford, usually by car but sometimes by train where there was a choice of two different routes. I was learning the intricacies of the textile trade, including the art of cutting cloth with a mechanically operated knife. I tendered for some contracts including over-alls and boiler suits for the Leeds Corporation dustmen and other employees. Rather to my surprise I obtained this contract, which like many others I found difficult to complete at a profit. I felt it was good to be learning the intricacies of manufacturing and trading, but I did not see the day coming in the immediate future when I would be showing a profit.

At my suggestion Norma returned to the Leeds University Institute of Education, as she had failed in her exam at the end of the year when I too was there. She claimed the failure in the exam was due to my distracting her from her work at the University. At all events when she took the exam again two years after the previous occasion, she passed easily.

I became rather tired of commuting between Leeds and Bradford, and decided that I must be one of the few people who was familiar with the two rather different cities. Eventually we started looking for a house which would be convenient for both cities, and decided that Pudsey and Guiseley were almost the only possible places. We liked Guiseley (which lies between Leeds and Ilkley) better than Pudsey, and eventually found a house to our liking at Tranmere Park, Guiseley, near the road which led to Bradford.

Luckily I had the benefit of a Trust which my father had made, and which was entitled to buy a property for my benefit. I wrote to them suggesting that No. 3 The Crescent, Tranmere Park, Guiseley, Leeds, was what we wanted to buy, and asked if the Trust would buy it on our behalf. From their reply it appeared that they would be willing to buy, and after inspections and a certain amount of time had elapsed, the Trust bought the house for about £5,000.

After this we were able to sell No. 4 Regency Court, Leeds, which I had bought with my own money, so on the balance I was able to show a profit at least on my property transactions but my efforts to show a profit in running my business had so far been unsuccessful, so I carried on with the business but hoped I would be able to sell it if opportunity arose.

Meanwhile Norma's father had been appointed Manager of a Co-operative Society bakery in Bradford, and my in-laws the Harris's were looking for a house in Bradford, which they eventually found at Rooley Lane, a new road on the side of a hill at one of the entrances to the town.

When my in-laws moved to Bradford they were closer to our new home at Guiseley, and started coming over to see us at fairly frequent intervals. We also went over to see them at their house at the other side of Bradford. I began to wonder if my wife was seeing rather a lot of her parents, who might be giving her advice to interest herself rather more in the welfare of her parents than in her own family and her husband's — an unfortunate development.

So life continued throughout the late 1950s and early 1960s. We were glad to welcome the addition to our family of a son, Alan, and a daughter, Helen. I was quite enjoying life in Yorkshire, though my business still remained unprofitable and I began to work quite hard in the fairly large garden of our house at Guiseley.

My father's Trust, who actually owned the house at Guiseley, gave no trouble and I wondered how they would react to the suggestion of buying another property, probably in Scotland. I began to feel that I wanted closer to my own family, and also to wonder what it would be like to live actually in Scotland. I felt that if I was ever to live independently in

My wife, Norma, with Alan and Helen at our home in Yorkshire, 1963.

Scotland it had better be soon, while I was still fairly young, and able to cope with any new problems and experiences. I mentioned these ideas to my wife, and she seemed to be in sympathy. She had had a school teacher who came from the Isle of Man, and had succeeded in interesting her very much in the Isle of Man and its history. She was ready to accept Scotland as another country like the Isle of Man with a long history and a Celtic background. In fact my wife always seemed to take a romantic view of any situation, and she was willing to look at Scotland through romantic glasses just as she had the Isle of Man.

We began taking holidays in Scotland, usually in areas fairly close to the English border such as Langholm in Dumfriesshire, or New Galloway in Galloway. After the visit to New Galloway I ordered the "Galloway News" to be sent to me every week in Guiseley, and studied in particular the property advertisements.

One day there appeared in the Galloway News an advertisement of a small estate for sale, some 250 acres with a farm, woodlands and mansion house. I answered the advertisement, put in by a firm of solicitors in Castle-Douglas, and received particulars of the estate which was situated by the big stretch of water known as Loch Ken or River Dee beside the road from Castle-Douglas to Ayr.

This advertisement certainly aroused my interest. Being on the road from Castle-Douglas to Ayr it was about 36 miles from my father's house, to which he had retired having handed over the family estate to my brother. He decided to look at the estate, in particular the mansion house, to see if we could possibly live there or re-build it to our satisfaction.

I may say that I was keener on the project of moving to Galloway in South-West Scotland than my wife, but she agreed to consider it as a possibility. We looked over the estate and decided that the mansion house was not in a good state of repair and certainly would be expensive to run. But I said it would be possible to demolish the mansion house and build a smaller house in its place. The woodlands seemed to be fairly mature, made up of a mixture of beech, oak and pine, with other species all of which were ready to be cut down and sold. This would go far towards off-setting the purchase price of the estate.

The purchase price of the estate in fact was rather low, about £20,000 for the 250 acres together with sporting and grazing lands along the loch-side which belonged to the South of Scotland Electricity Board. Altogether the property was a bargain, which perhaps did not appeal to some people as they would have to alter or re-build the house before moving into it.

However, I felt that I could re-build the house, if necessary. I would be willing to work to make the estate a profitable concern. My wife agreed with me.

I wrote to the trustees and asked them whether they would be willing to buy the estate on my behalf. They replied that subject to a surveyor's report, they would do so. It seemed to me that I had found a worth-while undertaking.

My trustees began to consult with solicitors in Edinburgh with a view to buying Parton Estate. Not long afterwards a man came into my factory in Bradford and asked if I was the owner of it. I replied that I was.

"How much does tha want for the place, lad," said the man, who said he was a wholesale butchers' supplier. He had the rights of using a new kind of extra strong white nylon cloth which would do very well for butchers' over-alls. How much did I want for the business?

"About £1,000," I said, naming what I thought was a reasonable figure. "Alright lad," he said. An inspiration came to me. "What about the stock?" I said. "How much does tha want for that, lad?" he said. "£600," I replied. "Alright lad," the gentleman replied. "Will thee make up some over-alls for me in this material."

I agreed to do as he wanted, and my machinists found the material very hard, thick and difficult to work. However, we managed it, and I had an agreement of sale drawn up between me and the purchaser. He paid me, and I handed him the possession, thankful to leave the slum-like and disagreeable Lumb Lane area of Bradford. I had not been able to make a profit out of textiles, and as it turned out the future for the textile trade in Britain was extremely black. I heard that my successor eventually went bankrupt. The machinists, "girls" as we called them, did not think that the new buyer would be a pleasant man to work for, which would make things more difficult for him. I decided that I was well out of the whole project.

I still had several months to wait at Guiseley before a definite agreement was drawn up between me and the trustees as to the terms on which I was to have Parton Estate, near Castle-Douglas. I wrote to the trustees that I would not move to Parton until they gave me the lease of the estate in legal terms. Some time after this they wrote that they had bought the estate and would hand it over to me as the owner.

While we were waiting for a final decision to be made regarding Parton Estate, I obtained a position as assistant to a Private Detective in Bradford. The private detective had a most alluring, dark-haired secretary, but I do not know how close the relationship was between them. He seemed to be a cold, calculating, efficient person, although fairly pleasant and amiable in conversation with me. I do know that my employer and his secretary were willing to provide evidence in divorce cases, of a kind that seemed necessary according to the law of the time.

According to the English law then, one of the easiest ways of obtaining divorce was on the grounds of adultery, and it was not usual in the courts to ask for more than a statement from one of the parties to the marriage and another person of opposite sex that adultery had taken place. Usually the non-guilty partner in the marriage would not, or could not, oppose the adultery claim.

My employer, or his secretary, were willing to, and not infrequently did, keep an assignation with a party seeking a divorce, and subsequently gave evidence in court that adultery had taken place. Subsequent easier divorce legislation made all this unnecessary.

Besides a secretary, my boss employed two other girls to keep an elaborate filing system, in which all judgments of debt against individuals in the area were recorded, and also the details and results of innumerable hire-purchase agreements. The boss employed too another man, an assistant and office manager, besides myself. My chief job, as it turned out, was to go round Bradford and district, mainly in the large council-owned housing estates, checking and recording details in connection with hire-purchase applications. Sometimes I made calls to collect money where it was due, or note the result of my visit. Indeed matters of debt form quite a large industry in Britain and no doubt all other countries.

Finally the day drew near for our move to the estate in South-West Scotland, which in a way was to have fairly momentous effects.

3

Twenty Years On

We moved to Parton House, near Castle Douglas in South-West Scotland, in 1966, although the estate had actually been bought for me by my father's trustees in 1964. We had decided to demolish the existing Mansion and replace it with a smaller one, as it was old-fashioned (built late mid nineteenth-century), not in the best state of repair, and partly damaged by a previous fire.

The demolition cost £2,000 and £1,000 was recovered by a sale of stone and contents. I found that the Trustees considered they had spent enough on the estate (though it was something of a bargain at £20,000) and that further expenditure had to be met personally by me, largely out of another of my father's Trusts which had come into my hands.

Finding that my resources could be considered limited, the scope for building a new Mansion was rather reduced and finally we chose a Colt cedar design of house. We chose one of the larger designs from the Colt catalogue, a two-storey building with two bathrooms, six bedrooms of varying sizes and numerous "modern conveniences".

Our new house was quite quickly erected on the old foundations, at a total cost I reckoned at £9,000. It has a commanding site on a bank overlooking Loch Ken, which is a considerable if fairly shallow body of water some ten miles long. It seemed advisable to cut down much of the existing mature woodland which brought in £7,000 — this however was largely spent on the replanting.

I was able to start achieving one of my long-lived

ambitions, which was to explore the hill country of Galloway. Parton House, though not high itself, is within a short car drive of the heart of the Galloway Hills. I was able to join the Galloway Mountaineering Club, based mainly in Dumfries, and in fact after a length of time I became for some three years its President.

The Galloway Hills are a remarkably rugged and extensive area whose highest point is The Merrick, at 2770 feet (843 metres) the highest point in Scotland South of the Highlands. Much of the Galloway Hills area is steep and rocky and it contains many Lochs or Lakes. One of these, Loch Enoch, is at 1617 feet far higher than any other loch as large (or larger) in the whole of the British Isles.

Our two children, now growing up, were not much more than babies when we arrived at Parton. I remember Alan, when he first saw many sheep, cried out "dog, dog, dog" as he was presumably more used to dogs than sheep at our Yorkshire home. It was noticeable that Norma, my wife, took a greater interest in our first-born son than in our daughter. In fact she "petted" him so much that in the long run it probably did him harm, whereas our comparatively neglected daughter was inspired to overcome her smaller size and develop into the beautifully proportioned wife that she now is.

My wife regarded her parents as a great responsibility, eventually securing for them a house in Dumfries to which they moved from Yorkshire. Here her father obtained a position as a master baker, and my wife began to work in Dumfries, becoming a teacher at the High School. Although the theoretical aspects of teaching did not interest her greatly she soon became an excellent practical teacher and was invited to move to Dumfries Academy, where she eventually became (though always a part-time teacher) Deputy Head of the Classics Department.

By comparison with to-day, the nineteen-sixties were known as a time of "full employment". Wages, and I think inflation too, were rising rapidly and it was more difficult for employers to find suitable employees than it was for people to find jobs. The firm of factors or land agents who helped me administer the estate had engaged a man as estate worker and forester who in his youth had apparently been reputed to be the worst boy at his local secondary school. He had a wife and a large family, and when we arrived was occupying one of the half dozen or so estate houses. The family had a rather ragged appearance; there was a time when the parents stood outside their house throwing a tin of baked beans forwards and back at each other.

My employee was very strong, but when one day he seized me by the lapels and shook me I decided it was time to give him his notice. I had a succession of forester/estate workers, most of them leaving me, but their quality seemed to gradually improve.

The general state of the buildings, dykes and fences and of the estate generally was poor. I began to improve the buildings, mend the dykes, surface the drives and improve the estate generally. I had some help from my father, who was particularly interested in an old Listed Building on the estate. This was built about 1580 as a Priest's House by the Glendinnings of Parton, who then owned the estate.

The Priest's House is a most attractive white-washed building which later became the Gardener's House when the next owners, the Murrays, constructed a three acre Walled Garden next to it. The Priest's House, although a beautifully curved structure with elegantly shaped windows, had no kitchen but only a living room/kitchen opening directly off the front door. My father provided funds which enabled a kitchen wing to be added to the house, and other improvements made (such as a bathroom).

I needed some road-metal for the estate's roads and was advised to get in touch with Mr Gibb, the County Council's Works Director and manager of its Quarry near Kirkcudbright. I found Mr Gibb to be a formidable but likeable figure who by many was regarded as effectively THE County Council in its relations with many of the public.

Although I was dealing effectively with Mr Gibb and his subordinates, I became curious as to the nature of the Kirkcudbright County Council which seemed to be such a remote and ineffective body. When I heard that the Councillor for Parton and Crossmichael was about to retire, I decided to put myself forward for the position. All that was needed was a Proposer and Seconder, and for these I was able to obtain two fairly influential local figures. Nobody else came forward to oppose me, so I found myself duly elected to Kirkcudbright County Council.

By this time (it was 1970) I considered that I knew the

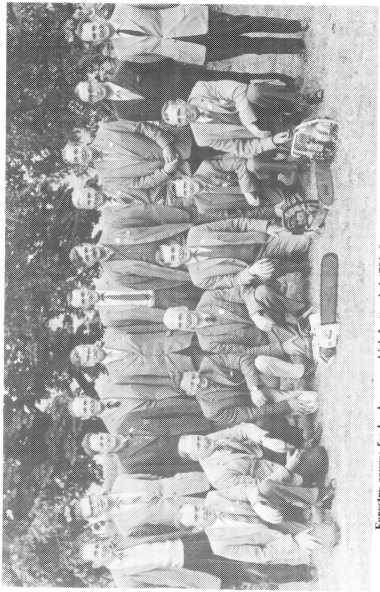

Forestry course for landowners which I attended (fifth from left on rear row) circa 1968.

Parish of Parton, with its widely-scattered population, fairly well, but I could not say the same about Crossmichael. Crossmichael is a large village, with a population of some 1,000, on the main road North four miles out of Castle Douglas.

I went to see the retiring or retired Councillor, and asked him to tell me something about Crossmichael. "Oh," he said. "It's just a dormitory town for Castle Douglas. If I were you, I wouldn't take Crossmichael too seriously."

Armed with this advice, I went to take my seat in the Council Chambers at Kirkcudbright. It turned out there were several new Councillors, and there was also an Inspector of Police who was supposed to show us round the building. "Don't ask me," he said, "I'm new here myself."

One of the first things that struck me about the Council was the importance of Colonels. The Convenor (or Chairman) was Colonel Batchelor, who had commanded the King's Own Scottish Borderers during the war and by 1971 was being described as "senile". His deputy was Colonel Ross, a formidable figure who was the effective disciplinarian on the Council. Colonel Ross was also Chairman of the Education Committee, which made him a feared figure among the teachers. Another important figure was Colonel Clark Kennedy, who seemed to represent part of the Galloway Hills area.

I did not quite know where to sit, so took what seemed to be an empty and reasonably well placed chair. Later I was reproached for this. "You are a Glenkens Councillor", I was told (the Glenkens include much of the hilly part of Kirkcudbrightshire.) "The Glenkens councillors sit over there." He pointed to a rather remote corner. However I managed to keep my original place, not without difficulty.

The County Clerk, a friendly father figure, asked me which two Committees I would like to join. I said Housing and Social Work. This was agreed to.

A popular pursuit with Scottish Landowners is shooting, and at this time I was quite keen on shooting. Sometimes I organized the shooting on my estate myself, and at other times I let it for quite a large sum. Besides shooting on my own estate, for the first few years I spent in Galloway I joined a Shooting Syndicate a good few miles away to either East or West.

Shooting of pheasants, grouse, deer, geese or other game plays an important part in the British countryside, and of course elsewhere too. Parton estate is renowned for the geese and duck to be found there and there is a good stock of pheasants which can be added to by semi-artificial means. I joined two shooting syndicates at different times, one in Wigtownshire and the other on the Duke of Buccleuch's land which shot mainly grouse with some other game too.

My wife continued to feel very strongly her responsibility towards her parents. She bought them a house in Castle Douglas, towards which I contributed financially without receiving any thanks from her. About this time, or a few months earlier, my wife began to be bitten by what I personally would call the "bug" of feminism.

My own view of feminism, for what it is worth, is that it is largely a reaction against the way men have treated women in the recent past, rather than a part of what might be called "natural justice" or an example of how things are moving which may be expected to remain in a feminist pattern for many long years to come.

In my view there is a natural way for men and women to regard each other and to behave towards each other, which has been disturbed and falsified by the way in which men have actually tended to behave towards women at certain times in the past. At present, it seems to me that it is women who are tending to behave towards men in an unnatural fashion. My hope is that in the long run reason and good sense will prevail, and that men and women will tend to behave towards each other in what could be called the natural and civilized masculine and feminine way.

My wife began to adopt more and more a feminist point of view, tending to contradict and disagree with me in which I may say she was encouraged by her parents and even to some extent by our children.

Eventually my wife gave up her teaching at Dumfries Academy, where she was highly regarded, and started to do what had apparently been one of her ambitions for a long time past. She was "incurably" romantic in outlook and it seemed had always wanted to write romantic historical novels. She started to do this; in quite a short time she had one typed ready for the publisher. I may say it was me who suggested the title for it, for which I had little thanks.

"Dark Justice" was submitted to Mills & Boon, who rejected it, and then to Robert Hale, who accepted it. My wife immediately began writing a second historical novel, while Dark

Justice was being published and apparently selling reasonably well.

Writing romantic historical novels became the activity having priority in my wife's life although she did not neglect her house, her parents, or her children. She was particularly successful in promoting her daughter's education, first to Crawfordton House school in Dumfries-shire and then to St. Denis School in Edinburgh. Much of the children's education cost was paid by my father, who never lost his sure touch with investments in stocks and shares. I am glad to say I have inherited this a little, but to a lesser degree.

Eventually my wife completed and sold four historical novels in two years, a feat which seemed to wear her out. She had a tendency to suffer from anorexia, or lack of appetite and of eating. Her diet too was unsatisfactory, very much lacking in bulk. Being the daughter of a baker (after the war she had actually driven delivery vans and sold bread) she had something of a reaction against bread, eating very little of it and delighting in feeding it to the birds. Her favourite food was meat, which actually provides good food value in little bulk. A largely meat diet made Norma excessively thin, and of course bulk and roughage is an important part of diet. Her doctor used to refer to her, with her carnivorous diet, as a "greyhound".

Norma began to become ill, with an illness which eventually proved fatal. Like her father (and unlike me) she had poor circulation. Her illness, I believe, was akin to leukaemia.

Another unhappy time in my life was upon me. I had never forgotten my six years as a journalist in Fleet Street. While living in Galloway I tried to become known by the local journalists and newspapers. I made a fair number of paid contributions to newspapers, as well as writing "letters to the editor". However earning a living as a free-lance journalist has become much more difficult in recent years. Newspapers have much less money to spend and what they do have they spend on their own staff rather than on outsiders.

At first I enjoyed being a member of the County Council. I actually joined the Parton Conservative Association, although in England I had generally voted Liberal. However when I went to the Annual General Meeting of the Galloway Conservative Party at Dalbeattie what I considered to be stupid points of view put forward by stupid people put me off being a Conservative.

I did not renew my subscription to the Parton Conservative Association. Instead I began to be sympathetic towards the Scottish National Party, which was making progress in Galloway as elsewhere in Scotland. It returned a Member of Parliament for Galloway and eleven M.P.'s in Scotland in the 1974 General Election.

The Kircudbright County Council, as in other Scottish rural counties up to that time, seemed to me to be dominated by ex-officers, landowners and farmers. There was a farmer who supplied milk of inferior quality, and the Council decided yet again (against my advice) to give him "one more chance".

I attended a meeting of the Scottish Landowners' Federation at a Gatehouse-of-Fleet hotel. Sitting together for lunch at a table in the centre of the dining-room were Colonel Batchelor, Colonel Ross and Colonel Clark-Kennedy. I remarked that it reminded me of a play then popular in London called "The Love of Three Colonels". This remark though it produced laughter, probably did not make me more popular with the Conservative element on the County Council.

I became more friendly with the younger and more left-wing element on the Council, usually lunching with them at the Selkirk Arms Hotel, Kirkcudbright. The friendly, father figure of a County Clerk had retired, his successor being an official who had trained as a lawyer and adopted a legal rather than paternal attitude towards Council business.

It transpired that one of the younger Councillors was about to resign and take up a new job in Aberdeen. He was a teacher who found it difficult to attend day-time Council meetings and wanted them to take place in the evening. Most of the Councillors were employers or retired people who were able to attend meetings during the day.

The Editor of the local newspaper had also retired recently, which resulted in an old friend of mine being succeeded as Editor by a man whom I did not yet know at all well. Unwisely I rang him up and told him that a young Councillor was resigning with some bitterness and moving to Aberdeen.

It appears that the new Editor broke an old tradition of Press confidentiality and told the new County Clerk that I was giving away Council secrets to the Press (I may say that I had never been given any kind of official instruction as to what Councillors should and should not do). The County Clerk passed on the news to the County Convenor, who wrote me a hand-written note suggesting that in the circumstances I ought to resign.

This new situation, together with my wife's illness, made me unhappy. I sought legal advice in Castle Douglas, and on the whole the legal advice given me was not helpful. I decided I might as well resign, seeing that I seemed to be making enemies in all directions.

My ultimate resignation, though I considered the matter for a while, caused my wife rather to lose confidence in me. She said that she supposed she ought to stand for the Council in my place, though I was doubtful whether her particular talents, and poor state of health, qualified her to be a successful Kirkcudbright County Councillor. From then on, I think, although she continued to write novels in what I thought might be a slightly feverish fashion, her health continued to decline. She died in hospital in December, 1972.

I have always been, I think, a rather religious kind of person. At school I enjoyed Chapel services, as a welcome break from the hurly-burly of school life, and I think I really found interesting the religious topics and studies which were put before us. I enjoyed and found interesting Scripture lessons, even the study of the original Greek New Testament which I undertook in one of the higher forms or class-rooms. I obtained a School Certificate Credit in Scripture, which included the optional study of one of the books of the New Testament in Greek.

From time to time throughout life I have found religious experience to be particularly close to me, and I will try to mention one or two of the outstanding religious experiences which I have had. I have already told in my first pages of the strange return from apparent death which I had at the age of nine.

Several times in my life I have felt that God is particularly near, that He is speaking to me or even that He is entering into me.

After my resignation from the Council and my wife's death my life seemed to have gone into a state of gloom and depression. I have generally found the months of February to April the most depressing of the year, until Spring comes. There was some sympathy for me when I left the Council — the general saying about the area was that I had "blotted my copy-book".

The only thing was to concentrate on the Estate and business affairs. I had a rather strange letter from my sister-in-law in New Zealand, where she had married and had two young sons. She said she would willingly look after my two children for me, presumably in New Zealand.

However I never had the least doubt that I would look after the two children myself, as indeed I have done with fair success. I have always been told that they have been particularly pleasant children to meet. They seem even up to this day to find their father quite a useful person in their lives.

My wife had taken on as a kind of help in the house the wife of a "second forester" whom I had engaged, and who told me that his wife could help in the house and kitchen. When my wife died I doubled this lady's wage, and told her she could come to the house quite frequently as a cook-housekeeper. She is to this day an excellent cook, and I certainly found her services valuable.

In 1973 there occurred "the first great oil price rise crisis". Jordan, the Arab ally of Great Britain, was threatened with invasion by Syria. It looked as though the forces of Jordan, Syria and Israel might meet near Megiddo or the biblical Armageddon, which in biblical prophesy has been regarded as the site of the great struggle which would foretell the end of the world. I told the Scottish Daily Express that this seemed to me a possibility and they seem to have passed on my view to the Foreign Secretary, Lord Home. As a result British troops reinforced Jordanian forces, who repelled the Syrians and ejected the Palestinian Liberation Organization from the country.

Lord Home's forceful moves, which were not exactly what I had anticipated, offended the whole Arab world and led to action by the Arab-sponsored Organization of Petroleum Exporting Countries. They raised oil prices by 70%, then by another 130%. This had a catastrophic effect on world economies in general, and no doubt contributed to the fall of the Heath Government in Britain.

So I suppose I can claim to have played a significant part in world affairs.

I have never specially enjoyed the celibate life. So at a suitable passage of time after my wife's death I began to wonder if I could find a replacement. I suppose I am more difficult to please than I was in more youthful days, and I am aware that I am not exactly equivalent to every woman's dream man (if indeed there is such a person!) "Once bitten, twice shy" goes the old saying, and I am aware of the difficulties that can follow a marriage or even a friendship. Still, while there's life there's hope, and I have indeed had a variety of experiences.

I was struck when I met a beautiful girl called Jonet at a party, and immediately started writing a poem about her (it is printed later in this book as "To Jonet, of Duns"). I have remained friendly with Jonet, but she is perhaps a girl who thinks that her own beauty and position in life can give her all she wants, which did not seem to appear to include a husband and children.

No doubt I have met other girls and women from time to time, and entered into various degrees of relationship with them, but so far it has not included engagement or marriage. Still, I may as well observe here that I am "open to offers" from the opposite sex, although I do not know exactly which kind of offer I would necessarily accept, or from what kind of person.

There have been moments when I have been depressed about Parton Estate, or at any rate the financial side of it. The expenses of running an estate nowadays tend to exceed the income obtainable from it, and this seems to be especially true with regard to Forestry at least in my case. Home-grown timber in Britain seems to fetch a much lower price than imported timber, to an extent that can hardly be justified. In the case of my area, and other areas, the length of transport to market seems unnecessarily long and expensive. Could more timber-using industry be set up locally? There is certainly much timber available in our Region for it.

While my wife was still with me I started writing poetry again (I had not done so since my earliest youth) and I eventually produced a reasonably large amount. The last chapter of this book contains these poems, some of which have religious significance. I like to think that as well as being attractive they contain some interesting thoughts and are applicable to present problems.

During much of my life I have had a sensation that something akin to miracles was, or could or might be, taking place all around me. Two of the most striking examples occurred in the Scottish Highlands.

For a time I joined the Institute of Directors, describing

my enterprise as Parton Estate Company. On one occasion the Institute of Directors arranged a week-end for its members on special terms at a Highland Hotel or Country Club called Knockie Lodge.

Knockie Lodge is situated not far from the South Bank of Loch Ness, being separated from the Loch by a wooded stretch on an upward slope, at the end of which Loch Ness is visible at the bottom of a steep wooded bank rising one thousand feet or so from the Loch.

There is in fact a track which leads from Knockie Lodge through the wood and down the bank to the loch, which is used by those wishing to go boating or fishing. However, I had left the track, intentionally or otherwise, and thrust my way through the young fir trees until I came to the top of the bank, after which I picked my way down the steep slope to the loch. Then I climbed up the bank again.

I found myself in a thick part of the wood, with no indication where to go except that through the young, thick firs I could see a high hill rising a few hundred yards away, which I knew was a direction to avoid. I stumbled through the wood without making any progress. Later that morning I recorded the whole episode in my diary as follows.

"I lost my way among the young trees on the 1,000 feet climb from Loch Ness back over the top of the ridge to Knockie Lodge where I was staying.

A hill loomed up ahead of me which I knew I should not climb. On all sides the trees seemed to obscure the way.

I prayed to God in my difficulty and I was told that He would send an angel to walk beside me and guide me. I could not see the angel but felt he was there. A new way through the trees seemed to appear and we walked along that way. After about 300 yards a regular track came into view which proved to be part of the road by which I had started into the forest from Knockie Lodge.

Quietly the angel slipped away and I was back in a known place.

Finally two aeroplane trails made a Cross in the sky.

Eventually the Cross changed into a St. Andrew's Cross across the sky."

The other mystic experience which I have had in the Highlands is described in one of my poems.

In November, 1985 my father died at the age of 96 and I

suppose I succeeded to his title becoming Sir Edward Hunter-Blair, 8th Baronet. I have not renounced this title, and am willing to accept it for what it is worth.

How do I foresee the future? As I indicated earlier in this book I am not specially optimistic and doubt whether technology and Science can in themselves necessarily provide for us an ever-improving future. In my first chapter I quoted from the work of Professor C. S. Lewis where he speaks of "truncated" thought, which is in fact connected with what we call the "scientific" habit of mind. So I would say that our "scientific" habit of mind, if that is what we take pride in, should be tempered as necessary by habits of Logic and Philosophy. C. S. Lewis advances reasons for believing that a supernatural element is present in every rational man. In fact, in his view, Nature as a whole is herself one huge result of the Supernatural; God created her.

Modern man, both modern scientific man and modern semi-scientific man, have perhaps become too complacent and self-satisfied about ourselves. Selfishness and self-satisfaction are perhaps not as rewarding after all as those who believe in them think.

Weapons of destruction — and especially atomic weapons — seem to be now so destructive that they would cause irreparable or almost irreparable harm.

The English-speaking peoples seem to be adopting a more and more lazy manner of speech which is preventing them from ever being able to learn any other language. Many English people to-day hardly open the mouth or use the lips firmly in speaking at all. The state of modern language teaching and learning in British schools to-day is generally agreed to be deplorable.

Standards of spelling and so on in British newspapers and documents are also falling.

The vast mass of the world's population to-day feel thwarted, under-developed and hoping for a change. Communism/Socialism is the most obvious stick for them to cling to as they drown in their ocean of ignorance and poverty. Indeed most people in the world to-day would probably accept Communism if it was thrust upon them.

Traditional Conservatism, with its hard outlook and division between "us" and "them" may be nearing the end of its reign in Britain at least. Recent opinion polls seemed to show that British Conservatives were sinking more and more into becoming an unpopular and disliked minority. To the rest of Europe British Conservatives tend to seem alien.

Perhaps Britain is suffering from the invention of the aeroplane. Insularity, which helped England so much from the sixteenth to early twentieth centuries, no longer seems, perhaps, useful or possible.

Science and technology may help the West to maintain its hold for some time to come; but on the other hand they may not.

On a final note of hope, there may be a benevolent, invisible to us power, behind us which will serve us however great (within limits) our sins and faults become. Yet I feel that there must be limits to God's forgiveness, and who are we to know where these limits are?

My daughter Helen and I on holiday in Greece circa 1980.

4

Philosophical Anthropology

Since I completed the previous chapter in this book I have had occasion to study Philosophical Anthropology, which seems to me to contain important messages for mankind in general and possibly for me in particular.

My study of Philosophical Anthropology is based on a lengthy entry in the 15th edition (1985) of the Encyclopaedia Britannica, of which fortunately I possess a copy.

Man has a nature, it is stated, widespread and persistent, that is obviously characteristic of his kind and notably different from the natures of other living things. Scholarly or scientific disciplines do not present it in terms of all that common sense recognizes in it.

"You can't change human nature," was a phrase I used to hear. This is still a subject of controversy — there are those who believe in the power of education or of learning or of conditioned response to modify original nature, and those who say that such man-caused evils as war and crime are rooted in particularities of an unalterable inborn nature.

The modern discipline of Philosophical Anthropology had its origin in the 1920s, although Western Philosophy has been concerned with man since the 5th century B.C.

The Middle Ages, while they had no discipline of anthropology in the strict sense, did have a section of theology that concerned the fallen nature of man and the possibility of salvation, which was offered to him by divine Grace in accord with the redemption offered by Christ.

The Renaissance had the effect of removing Man from

the ascendancy exercised over him by cosmic discipline or divine authority. Without rejecting the presence of God, man became a centre of interest in his own eyes.

Blaise Pascal (1623-1662) the French scientist and religious writer, described man as neither angel nor beast and said it was therefore fruitless to try to understand him as a fallen god or as an animal raised to a higher state.

The 18th century Enlightenment thinkers rediscovered that man is not only a natural being, but also a cultural being. It seems to me that we in Britain rather fail to live up to the definition of man as a natural and "cultural" being. On the cultural side, the standards of the mass of the British population are rather low, and probably getting lower.

The immense progress of the social sciences was one of the significant aspects of the history of thought in the 19th century. Nevertheless the specialists in these sciences — and in all the human sciences — became more restricted and specialized in their outlook. They made excessive pretensions for their own sciences but were prisoners of their specialization, unable to view man in his totality or in his essence. The specialist in the religious sciences saw everywhere only ritual behaviour; the specialist in economics reduced all individual or social life to preoccupations with material self-interest.

Philosophical anthropology developed as a remedy for this epistemological anarchy by maintaining, in contrast to the empirical sciences, the primacy of values in an understanding of man. Scientific endeavour, it held, is indispensable, but philosophical reflection has its place prior to and subsequent to the work of science. It must order the incoherent mass of results obtained from the sciences (to conform to the true essence of man). It is a reclaiming of human equilibrium in the rising tide of sciences and technologies.

The doctrine of evolution caused the previous view that species were stable to begin to be disbelieved, and the study and interpretation of fossils seemed to confirm this. The French naturalist Lamarck and the English Darwin (who wrote 'The Origin of Species') appear to have reviewed and corrected this school of thought.

Studies of the origin and development of the Universe, and of the origin and development of man, followed. There was controversy about man's origins, and indeed these matters of origin are still perhaps not finally resolved.

If man has a history of development, it is stated, then it must be recognized that man might continue to develop in the future. My own impression is that we are becoming taller, and perhaps growing up more quickly. And of course human population is increasing. These developments may or may not be dangerous, or beneficial.

Physical anthropology, it is said, is an integral part of cultural anthropology, and both are separate from philosophical anthropology. Max Scheler, a German philosopher, wrote in 1928 "I can state with some satisfaction that the problems of anthropology have become to-day in Germany the true centre of all philosophical studies."

Philosophical anthropology emphasises the individual human in his world. The individual does not benefit from complete freedom without limit (which perhaps allows for the concept of Law, or the State, or even God.) Materialism in all its forms tends to reduce personal existence. As well as a member of a group, each person is an individual.

Anthropology to some extent takes over from theology, and being human is capable of making mistakes. That "God is dead," as some thinkers have claimed, can, as others have said, lead to the claim that "man is dead" and that personal identity and individual existence are illusions.

The consequences of such views of humanity are negative and depressing. They seem to be the cause of attempts at genocide, or the haphazard development of a technological society that is threatening man with a new period of barbarism.

The task of philosophical anthropology, it is said, is to preserve the human meaning of human existence. For most philosophical anthropologists, it appears, a theological dimension is necessary to check threats that would destroy the image of man. Each individual consciousness must have the opportunity to discover its own views on his or her meaning, values and freedom.

One of the points I am trying to make in this book is the need for more study of the relationship between Philosophy, Religion and Science. Philosophical anthropology has some bearing on it. Religious eschatology, the study of Last Things, is I think still relevant. It could be more relevant than most of us think. What about the date 2,000 A.D., or alternatively two thousand years after the birth or death — and Resurrection — of Christ? (By the way, I believe there will be an eclipse of the sun visible in Cornwall in 1999).

There may still be a place for a Prophet in the world to-day, perhaps there is a vacancy waiting to be filled. If I were a preacher, I might consider if there is a need for redemption, on a collective and (or) an individual basis. Materialism may indeed have relevance to the world's present problems, but like Patriotism, of which Edith L. Cavell said "Patriotism is not enough," materialism too, as I see it, is "not enough."

5

Science and Religion: God exists

Here in Western Europe most of us live in some comfort, with our material needs fairly well provided for. But in the Third World, and elsewhere, that is not so.

Even when our material needs are satisfied, or if they are not, many of us still find we have questions not too easy to answer. Perhaps we read a newspaper or magazine, or attend church services, partly to help provide for our non-material needs.

In the past, religion helped to supply answers to peoples' questions and doubts on the non-material side of life. Nowadays religion seems sometimes to be of declining importance. Cannot Science answer the questions which religion seemed to supply answers to in the past?

And yet, there are still questions to which Science can hardly provide an answer. First, where did Early Man obtain his powers of reasoning and thinking, which gave him mastery over the beasts and ultimately brought him, for better or worse, to where he is to-day?

Second, how did Earth become such a perfect environment for life, when nothing else in the whole Universe seems to be suitable for life in any form?

Third, is there a future life, after this world?

Fourth, Science can work out laws for organic and

inorganic matter, but have there been exceptions, such as miracles, which seem to break these rules?

Fifth, ability to speak and use Language is unique to humanity. But we still do not known how languages began.

To some, including myself, the answer is most likely to be the part played by God, the creator. He made the basis for Life, and particularly Man. But we are not puppets, we have a choice in our actions. Yet God is capable of intervening, and does so from time to time.

Christians say that some 2,000 years ago God sent his son into the world, after having revealed himself in earlier times as told in the Old Testament. I was born late in 1920, and ever since I was a boy have had the feeling that some 2,000 years after Christ's birth or death there might be some further dramatic events in Man's history. We are running into possible danger (connected with nuclear weapons, or over-population, or environmental damage?) and if things go wrong God may or may not intervene in some way.

At Christmas 1987 I published a book of prose and verse, with photographic illustrations. It deals with autobiography, philosophy and religion and is published by Pentland Press, Kippielaw, Haddington, Edinburgh (Mr Douglas Law) at the modest price of £6.50. Its title is "A Mission in Life", and I think it may help provide answers to some of the questions I have raised in this article.

I wrote the above article with the intention of offering it for publication in a Sunday newspaper.

On considering it further, it seemed to me to indicate that there is no real opposition between Science and Religion. Science originated as a means of trying to find out the truth, by experimenting mainly with material substances. It also tried to study the World and the Universe, without any bias caused by previous prejudices and beliefs.

In recent times the boundary between the material and the non-material, from a scientific point of view, seems to be almost vanishing. In the ultimate analysis, matter seems to be little more than a number of electrical charges.

Scientists try to avoid making statements which cannot be proved. Religion, on the other hand, is largely a matter of Faith. Scientists can in fact be men (or women) of Faith, and religion. Two names that occur to me as showing this are Blaise Pascal and James Clerk Maxwell, and some of the Arab scientists and philosophers in the Middle Ages too.

In a rather modest way I have tried to be a scientist myself at times. Where I reside, in Galloway, there exist still some examples of fish of a type not common in Britain, the Charr (Salvelinus alpinus). They are really a relic of the last Ice Age, being land-locked, since British rivers are now too warm for them to descend to the sea as formerly.

My observations on the increasing rarity of charr in Galloway were noted by a well-known Freshwater Biologist, Dr Peter S. Maitland, and he has arranged for specimens to be transferred to lochs in a different part of Scotland. Although the charr is not uncommon in deep lochs in the Scottish Highlands, each separate population has acquired differences through long isolation from the sea.

Another interesting and attractive fish, which is facing extinction, is the Lochmaben Vendace, which is found only in Dumfries-shire. It may or may not be too late to transfer some specimens for preservation elsewhere.

While ~~Where~~ I do not claim to be a great scientist, I am certainly not against scientific endeavour. But by its very nature scientific endeavour seems to exclude the intangible, the higher forces which may have shaped our history and our lives.

I would only suggest that, so far, scientific experiment and religious forces have operated in different fields, without meeting. Whether they will meet, and in what form — and with what outcome, only a Prophet could foretell.

6

Some Poems

1984 — Not Orwell (Blair?)

I am perplexed about my life's future.
Or should it be my past, for I am old.
No, I believe it is my life's future.
The past has passed, and much will pass away.

I find it hard to concentrate on single things,
Like forestry, or gardening, or still less farming;
Or planning, or running my day-to-day life;
Or making friends, or social life affairs.

My interests are indeed too general.
I've rarely settled down to single aims.
A farmer's life requires a single aim,
To grow things as food, and sell them for money.

I cannot find a way to solve my problems.
I need a follower to go with me.
I thought I had a wife to go with me,
But she went away from me in her mind.

We are in a world of high technology,
And yet I think it has not solved our problems.
Production now can far outpace demand,
Production of goods, of food and even humans.

The British farmer sells his food with ease,
Thanks to a Common Agricultural Policy.

And yet supply here too exceeds demand.
Have we reached the time when Desire Shall Fail?

We live in a time of considerable suspicion,
Between East and West, and there is a Third World.
Are we nearing the final Armageddon,
Perhaps two thousand years after Christ's birth.

For a time there was a thing called Détente,
A relaxation of hate between East and West.
But that has gone. Why did it go? Why
Do we live in a world of a Nuclear Arms Race?

So I have problems. I am not alone.
The world, yes all mankind, is full of problems.
And the non-human sector has problems too,
One being that it cannot state or resolve them.

Why do we live and work and go on living?
Do we just earn our bread from day to day,
And carry on and create new generations
Until the time comes for our own personal release.

Yes, I think many of us do just that.
But to me at least it hardly seems enough.
And indeed I do not do it very well.
So I may as well continue my general thoughts.

What was wrong with Détente, and how did it end?
The Soviet Union wanted a relaxed relationship
With the West, less threats from nuclear weapons.
And for a time it seemed to achieve this aim.

We won a war in 1939-45,
And a previous war in 1914-18,
Against a German Reich with few allies
Which wanted to expand its rule over others.

But other countries and peoples disliked German rule.
They fought against it when they experienced it.
Large and powerful coalitions were formed
Which defeated the ambitious Germans and their allies.

Now we are faced with a war against Communism,
A Communism led by the Soviet Union.

plans

Our war ~~pains~~ against them are based on weapons,
On mighty forces and science and nuclear power.

Their plans against us are not based only on weapons.
Their weapons may or may not be equal to ours.
But Communism has an international appeal.
There are Communist parties and allies in many countries.

So we in the West (or at least at present the rulers)
Are frightened less of Communist might than doctrine.
We are frightened of Communism's popular appeal
In a fight for the minds and power over men.

It's not enough to have Détente and peace with Communism,
When times are hard and business is bad for the West.
For the East may win without much need for weapons,
By appealing to people who lack material prosperity.

So the West is mainly reduced to building up weapons.
And nuclear weapons, for they are the most powerful,
In case they cannot equal the East by peaceful means;
And besides, building weapons creates a kind of prosperity.

There is a demand for weapons of every kind,
In our own country and many other countries.
So it's possible to build up business and wealth
By producing arms and trying to sell them abroad.

In the long run, can this go on?
It can go on for a while.
But it must end either in Détente and peace
Or in military or moral victory for West or East.

I cannot prophesy which it will be.
And yet I would say there is one more alternative.
In Christian prophesy the Son of Man will return,
And the Kingdom of God will come to rule in glory.

The kingdom did not come in Jesus's lifetime.
It did not happen a hundred years,
Or five hundred years or a thousand years
After his birth, or even fifteen hundred years.

Soon it will be two thousand years.
I am mortal, I do not know.
And yet I think it could happen
In two thousand years.

Holiday Time

Hurtling through the night,
Past the blocks of light—
Buildings man has made—
    Runs the railway train.

Countrywide we roam,
On our journey home,
    Vacation's end again.

Summer light was dawning
In the early morning
    When we started out.

Pockets full of money
We made the long, long journey
    Through Carlisle, Birmingham.

Shouts of jubilation,
Taxi to the station,
    Cornwall, here we come.

A Future Time

And I saw a new heaven and a new earth
For the old heaven and the old earth
    Had passed away.
The earth was destroyed by nuclear war
    Between the nations.
And angels came and cleansed the earth
    With flaming swords.
I, Edward, sat above with God,
    With Father, Son and Holy Spirit.
The souls of the righteous were gathered around
    And there shall no torment touch them.

Was there a scattered remnant of humanity
Left, after the nuclear bombs had shattered earth?
    Perhaps, in some quiet corners
A scattered nucleus remained.
    A nuclear, or non-nuclear nucleus
Of men whose sin and overbearing pride

Was less than others' in this warring world.
Can they build up anew the broken piles
    Of those whose work is scattered on the ground?
They, with the heavenly host whose reign on earth
    Has now begun, may start to live afresh.

South-West Scotland

Ye Galloway hills, I like your name,
    Mullwharchar and Benyellary,
    Larg, Lamachan and Curlywee
Your ruggedness equals your fame.

Shalloch-on-Minnoch at the North
    Tarfessock, Kirriereoch too,
    Castle on Oyne and Rig of Milmore,
You bid the traveller go forth

To walk your rocks, your lochs, your glens
    Your tussock-grass and boggy flows,
    Your miles of lately-planted spruce,
Your hills less high than Highland Bens.

For many a rough and rugged mile
    I tramped on Cairnsmore, Rinns of Kells,
    Merrick (eight hundred and forty-three metres)
And now — I trust it was worth while.

Castle-Douglas Accordion and Fiddle Club

The fiddle and box
Can give many shocks
And lighten the spirits right well.

The spirits are there
And good Scottish fare
When we meet at Ernespie Hotel.

The music is great
Both early and late
In the evening at Castle-Douglas.

And Jacky Scott's there
As our cheerful compere.
Cares leave as the evening we pass.

J.R.

If a lady has great charm
Can she keep home and heart warm,
     I think so.

For a general goodness and grace
Go well with a pretty face
     In a loved one.

And if we are worthy too
What can the future do
     To upset us.

On the rock stands a tree:
Grace, strength in harmony
     lasting together.

To K.S., Wife of an M.D.

What is it like to be a doctor's wife?
It must be rather an unusual life.

Not far from every strange thing and alarm,
She keeps an air of dignity and calm.

The Second Coming

Deserted corners, abandoned people,
That is where the almighty goes.
Sweeping the corners, redeeming the people,
Fighting the devil and all his works.
Brightly lit corners, empty people,
There goes the devil to do his task.
Behind the brightly lit corners are sewers
Sewers of houses, sewers of people,
Owned by the devil and locked to God.

God is untiring, God lasts for ever,
Able to reappear in another form.
You know the Son, even the Holy Spirit,
Do you know everything, do you know God.

Elements of Fire

In the Middle Ages they spoke of four elements:
Earth, Air, Fire and Water.
Now scientists speak of many more elements:
"We are not living in the Middle Ages."

Would we be better off if we were?
At least we would have five hundred clear years ahead:
Years of progress, of gradual improvement.
But what have we now?

At the beginning darkness was upon the face of the deep.
Then there was light.
Ages later, life started in the waters
And the Age of Water began.

Life continued and developed in water,
Until at last some fishes moved to dry land.
With Insects, Plants, Amphibians, Reptiles,
The Age of Earth was in progress.

Then came the Age of Mammals and the Age of Man.
Still, life stayed on earth,
Until the twentieth century after Christ.
When it advanced into the Air.

The Age of Air had begun,
Say from 1915 A.D.
But it did not last very long,
Say until 1980 A.D.

Now we are living in the Age of Fire,
Of aerial bombing, of nuclear explosions,
Of terrorist actions, even nuclear war.
How long can this Age last?

The Age of Air lasted sixty-five years.
The Age of Fire could be shorter still,
To be followed by a Second Coming, an Armageddon.

Water, Earth, Air, Fire.
Have we moved from the Middle to the Last Ages?

Life is An Ice-Age Glacier

We are like boulders, born near a glacier
(Rubbed off from our mothers' wombs) . . . .

Rough, young, angular, I am full of my own ideas.
I explore the world around, am moved on a little by the infant
glacier below me.
I grow bigger, plants grow in my soil.
I put forth ideas and my features and limbs expand.
I move down from the mountain-top into the rough and tumble
of life.
I move around, am shattered by other rocks and revive again.
I learn wisdom, try to adjust myself to lie cunningly in relation
to the fierce icy forces around.

Perhaps if I am lucky I engage in a fertile relationship with
another rock.
We explore each other, we mate, is it a rock she gives birth to
or a human?
Slowly my angular corners are being rubbed off by the ice as it
moves along.
I become smoother, shiny, beautiful, at the height of my
powers.
My curly hair is like a field of Brussels sprouts.
I build, I grow, I create, I am reaped to benefit mankind.
I am rewarded with money to compensate for the first grey in
my hair.

And still I and all the other rocks move on and are ground
down by the glacier.
Some rocks grind down to nothing and some are thrown aside
to stagnate.
Time passes, we grow smooth and bald and small.
No longer do we grow crops and earn gold with our minds and
bodies.

If we are lucky we are thrown aside to be a monument in some
      foreign field,
Or pile up in a terminal moraine at the glacier's end.
Is this immortality, or a symbol maybe of immortality?

Is life like a journey on a glacier,
A combination of predestination and free-will?
Time will tell when all glaciers melt or cease to move.

Stands Scotland Where She Did

Stands Scotland where she did?
Probably not, but did she ever?
We never stand where we did.

      All is in motion,
      Moving staircases go forwards, backwards.

We take the staircases as they come.
We have a choice of what is offered.

      Forwards, backwards, for better or for worse.
      Little is gained by standing on the brink.

If we do not choose the choice is taken from us.
We end up worse off than before.
If we choose right we reach the promised land,

      Provided we tread the path and make it straight
      (We have to tread the path and smoothe it too).

Like a curler, throwing the Stone of Destiny,
There may be a man or woman to smoothe its way,
Or we must make its path and smoothe it too.

      Stands Scotland where she did?
      No, and she calls on us to smoothe her way.

Scotland's National Anthem

This should be sung to the tune 'Ye Banks and Braes o' Bonnie Doon' (verses 1, 3, 4) and 'Loch Lomond' (verse 2).

Ye banks and braes o' bonnie Doon,
    Ye banks and braes o' Galloway,
I hope with joy to see them soon
    And Burns's house at Alloway.

By yon bonnie banks and by yon bonnie braes,
    The bonnie, bonnie banks o' Loch Lomon',
O ye'll tak the high road and I'll tak the low road,
    And I'll see you in Scotland in the gloamin'.

Now we hae tramped the banks o' Doon
    And Gala Lane to Garrary,
We'll struggle on by licht o' moon,
    And meet all dangers manfully.

Beware of foes, steer clear of rocks,
    Let men and women real Scots all be,
Be ready both for joys and shocks,
    Then shall the world true Scotland see.

It is suggested that a 'National Walk' by Scots might go from time to time from Loch Lomond* across the Clyde, through Renfrewshire (Elderslie), Ayrshire (Mauchline, Burns country), to the River Doon, up to Loch Doon, along the Gala Lane river to Garrary Forest, past Loch Dee and finish at White Laggan bothy in the Galloway Hills — or possibly at the Bruce Stone by Loch Trool.

Alternatively the walk could take place in the opposite direction, say from Glen Trool or White Laggan to Balmaha on Loch Lomond.

This walk would symbolise the unity of 'Highland' and 'Lowland' Scotland, as does the National Anthem. The former Kings and Queens of Scotland often went on pilgrimage from Edinburgh to St. Ninian's shrine in South Galloway and the Scottish National Walk would I consider be this pilgrimage in present-day form.

Individuals might start from Edinburgh, Lerwick (Shetlands) and Stornoway, meeting by Loch Lomond to walk together to Galloway.

Perhaps from Ben Lomond.

To Jonet (of Duns)

There's a lovely girl called Jonet.
Has any-one written a sonnet
To her colour, flowing lines and chestnut hair?

Well, if not, I shall begin it
And dally for a minute
To see if I can enhance the beauty there.

She is like a pretty flower
That needs shelter from a shower
Of rain, and so I'll offer her my hand.

And if she comes with me
I am sure that she will see
That her problems only I can understand.

Galloway Hills

I sleep and I move in my feather-soft bed,
    By day I plough and plant the fields;
Or I travel round in my blue saloon
    Soliciting orders from customers.

Each weary hour of the dust-filled day,
    All through the heat of oppressive night,
I dream of each mile-long Galloway hill
    And Back Hill of Bush Cottage by moon-light.

For I have the key of the Garrary gate,
    The Garrary gate on the Forestry road,
The road that runs ten rough, long miles
    From Clatteringshaws to the cottage I seek.

Back Hill o' Bush is the heart o' the hills;
    A range lies behind and a range in front.
When I cross the granite-edged ridge ahead
    I shall face Mount Merrick so steep yet blunt.

I have woven the twisted thread of my life
    This way and that to cross-grained cloth.
Pleased am I with domestic lot,
    Yet would escape into solitude,

To stay in the bothy of Back Hill of Bush,
    By day crossing ranges of barren hills,
Moving through heather, the rocks and the lochs—
    But we must bear this present world of good and ills.

Daughter of King Ozymandias

Her name was Princess Ozymandia.
She dwelt in Ancient Egypt by the Nile,
In father's palace made of stone and brick
(Fashioned by slaves from river mud and straw).

The princess's wrists and ankles were so slim
That she but seldom played in lively games.
Her hair was golden, hanging down her back,
And she was fond of reading, music, art.

One day she sat and gazed upon the Nile,
Or made some music with an instrument,
Or chatted with a lady of the court
While resting in a little summer-house,

When suddenly a boat came down the Nile.
Out of it jumped a youth whose leg was hurt
So that he limped or hobbled on the grass,
And walked up to the princess and her friend.

"Please save me, girls," said he, "I am pursued
By soldiers and police, for I believe
That men are equal. Wealth and rank and class
Are but the surface dressing, like our clothes,
Which hide the real bare body underneath."

Then answered Princess Ozymandia,
"What is your name? I like your face, your ways,
And would discuss these things of which you speak.
Come hide yourself inside our summer house."

"My name is Chin," said he. They moved
The boat and hid it in some reeds.
And would that I had space to tell
Of all that happened after this:

How Ozymandia and Chin
Discussed the world at large
While Beth, the lady in waiting, too
Agreed to help his plans.

And how they tended him with care
And cured his wounded foot.
And fed him in the summer-house
For sixteen days and nights.

And how at last the princess left
With Chin, to take him home
To where he lived, not far away
In mud huts by the Nile.

And how she stayed there with his folk
And lived there many years
And married him, so all in all,
My tale is joy not tears.

A Mystic Experience

I saw a triangle on the mountain side
As I climbed Ben Lomond from Stuc a'Bhuic,
A triangle made up of three sheep,
For the Father, Son and Holy Spirit.
Two more sheep were Saints Peter and Andrew,
Two more Mary or Maureen and my son or daughter yet to be.
And a voice spoke to me in my head.
From now on you wear a halo.
Some day men may see it around your head.
God is you from today, or you are God.

I came to people walking along a track.
They looked neither to left nor right.
I shouted, but they heard me not.
Eyes have they, but they see not.
Ears have they and they hear not.
I passed a girl and she raised her eyes and spoke a little.
Then I walked on to the top of the mountain.
There I spoke to a man who had settled in Scotland,
English, lacking in ideas and knowledge.
Was he meant to tempt me, by Satan?

I made my way to the base of the mountain.
I went to the house of Stuc a'Bhuic.
It was empty, but clean and tidy within.
In its garden were seven Kniphofias,
Red and yellow, flaming, called Red-hot Pokers.
And four more in bud waiting beside them.
They were there to baptise me with fire.
Seven hot candles in seven candle-sticks
With four more in store for some future occasion.
I made my way down the road to my motor-car.

I raised my eyes to the top of the mountain.
A cloud, rather larger than a man's hand
Lay and covered the top of the mountain,
The greatest top on the right-hand side.
Behold the cloud moved to the next top beside it,
And then to the third of the tops of the mountain.
And then there were clouds on two of the three tops,
Each the size of one man's hands.
Father, Son and Holy Spirit,
Were sheep, then part of the rock of the mountain.

Ben Lomond in Scotland
July, 1977.

L.C.

Six hundred miles from home,
Amid the summer beauty and winter dark
Of Inverness, she stays, a living lamp
Of light, to brighten the dark night.

In winter, she is there. But will she stay?
When summer comes, maybe she'll spread her wings
And fly away like some bright butterfly
To distant fields, to love and mate maybe.

What cares she for the land she'll leave behind?
Some other nymphs will come and greet the crowd
Of visitors who flock around the nest
Where she now stays. But one

Will miss her and stay sadly in his home
Or maybe cry for other butterflies.

A Secret of Life

What is the secret of life? Could it be exploitation?
Are we always either exploiting or being exploited?
We live, we feed, we die, we are fed on.
Perhaps some exploitation of humans and animals is inevitable,
Even if too much exploitation fills me with disgust;
(Not, however, the exploitation of vegetables).

Suppose we hire others to join us, to do as we wish.
They demand more pay, to impose their will on us.
Or else we work for others, and obtain the best terms we can.
That is what is known as industrial relations.
Employees and employers should in principle co-operate,
And at worst must never forget their common humanity.

Sometimes I think I should live a life of comparative isolation,
So that none are affected by my faults and I do almost as I
please,
Knowing that my faults usually affect me more than others.
Or have I in fact had a bad influence on others, on the world,
Mainly because others have misunderstood my intention?
And the time will come when I really am dependent on others—
Health cannot last for ever, old age can take its place. Then at
least will I be content for others to exploit me,
And grateful I hope for help, disinterested or not.

Genesis, Or Revelation

And the earth was without form
And void.
And the Spirit of God moved
Or did it?
And the Universe began with a Big Bang,
Or less probably it is in a Solid State.
Science and Astronomy are considering these questions.
So far they have not given all the answers.
Cosmology and Earth Sciences are active.
Telescopes and radio telescopes bring new knowledge.
They have given no positive knowledge of God.
They have not said there is no God.

God created man in his own image
Says the Bible.
Be fruitful, and multiply,
And replenish the earth, and subdue it. . .
And have dominion . . . over every living thing.
So man carries out God's wishes.
Where will it end, and when?
Probably not for billions of years,
Say the astronomers.
What of earth's future?
That has its problems, say the ecologists.
Can man live according to Science?
Is materialism enough to make living worth while?
There is no definite answer at present.
If we ask such questions we must answer them ourselves.

True Thomas (The Rhymer)

Underneath the Eildon tree,
There shall I for ever be.

Till the time shall come again.
Then will I be seen by men.

And shall wed a mortal Queen.
Wondrous things may then be seen.

Until at last, all hand in hand,
We shall reach the Promised Land.

To W.B.

Life On The Rails

Railways — they solved the problem of moving around
In the nineteenth century. Building them was cheap
By present-day standards. Men shovelled and dug,
Thousands of them. Pay was low
By standards today, but not then. Railways contributed
To commerce, industry and in the end
To a great increase of population.

In Britain, and some other countries,
the importance of railways diminished
After about one hundred years.
Industrial activity spread world-wide
And in the founder countries, especially England,
Decline and over-population set in.

Oil, motor-cars and internal combustion engines
Became our constant environment and shell.
We travelled in steel cars, like a hermit crab in its shell,
Not able to park our cars any more than a crab its shell,
Poisoning the environment and breeding sub-normal children.

Now the environment is spoilt and petrol is over-expensive.
Costs rise, inflation proceeds and nuclear dumping threatens
To poison Scotland's hills for a hundred thousand years.
Will it be better to die in the quick shock of nuclear war,
Or slowly decline in the decadent years of a nuclear peace?

Revenons à nos moutons! Return to our railways (and sheep?)
Healthier ways can be found. Some there are who are finding
        them,
Living good lives without lead in petrol and water.
Western man must learn to co-operate like Southern and
        Eastern.
He must learn to move in a group in train or bus,
Not alone like a hermit crab in a hermit-shell of a car.

How much land have we handed over to motor-ways and
        lorries,
How much effort is wasted each year in over-maintaining roads,
So that lorries can rush past our houses
Excessively transporting goods?
Goods can go by rail and so can humans,
Binding our transport needs in a safe narrow ribbon of steel.

Now is the time for my muse to take wings of flight and
        allegory,
Sketching the life of man from a baby's cot to a grave,
Who is able to rise from the grave like a bird with angel's
        wings.

I need not tell you what happens at birth or conception.
Let us rather consider the infant asleep in his cot.
He may be forward or backward, advanced or retarded,

Healthy or ill, but always one thing is sure.
The baby depends entirely on those around him.

The little boy or girl has a need for food or drink,
Drinking only at first, then solid food also.
Guidance too the little one will absorb
From those who feed him and care for his infant needs.

Does John think for himself
Or take his ideas from those near him?
Environment counts for much in a young person's life,
Heredity too may signify.
Then there is a spark, a vital spark in all beings,

A vital spark in each one of us from the beginning,
Which separates man from the beast,
And gives to all humans a chance
To rise like a plant from the soil and put forth flowers
Of wisdom, of beauty, of strength and shed glory around.

Observe John and Jane who mature, in mind and body,
Influenced doubtless by friends, by parents and teachers.
As they grow up they choose. But their choice is limited.
None of us has unlimited choice in the way he shall go.

Like a train we set out from the station and reach the points,
The points in the track where the rails diverge from each other.
Each human train can choose which track to go on,
Uniquely privileged as we are to set the points
For good or bad, for arts, science or technology,
To be gregarious or solitary or homosexual or lesbian.

Each has his own set of choices, with none open to all,
Yet how we choose will set the tone of our lives.
Influenced by background and previous experience
We move from choice to choice or we reach a line
Which seems to lead on unchanging into the distance.

Paired or solitary, family folk or gregarious,
We pass from the dawn of life to the setting sun and the grave.

The Long Day

I saw an orb, as it were the sun,
All red at the rosy time of sun-rise.
From behind it came an infant,
Plump, cherubic, like a young Hercules.
Seemingly he sat himself upon a cloud
And drew a bow and arrows from a golden sling.
These arrows he shot towards the massive sun,
But his strength was as a child's, his aim poor.
Yet sometimes he would hit his mighty target —
Then the clouds thundered, the skies rang like bells
And it looked as if the child were handed a glass of lemonade.
He drank from the glass and as he drank he grew.
His strength increased, he drew more fiercely on the bow.
But as his strength grew the target drew away and became smaller,
Turning itself round a few degrees at the same time.
With each hit on the target the child grew
And at the same time the target changed whenever it was hit,
Growing smaller, colder, further away.
Behold it had changed from the sun into the earth,
The earth with its cities and fields of corn.
And the child was now a man, working
Like a man on the earth and feeding himself
From the fruits of his toil and the riches of the world.
He fed himself and in his spare time he married and multiplied.
Many men spread themselves about the earth. They exploited
The world, which began to diminish and grow cold.
Then I saw a man leave the earth upon a cloud;
Much like the man I had seen as an infant at sun-rise.
He drew a bow and fired at the setting sun.
His aim was good but his strength was beginning to decline.
He drew a reward from the sun, like unto glasses of red wine.
They nourished him, yet he became smaller and older.
His arrows were fewer and feebler, the target changing.
The old man gazed into the sun's setting ball.
He threw himself forward as it were on a heavenly stairway.
"Father, I come" he cried, to a heavenly welcome.

Epitaph

When I have died, let this be said of me,
    I never moved to any sheltered bay,
Running from challenges as they arose,
    But rather have I faced them. I have lived.

I have experienced all sorts of things:
    The inner and the outer human life:
Health, illness, labour, leisure, parents, sons,
    And being a man have lived with girl and wife.

I sympathise with everything I meet,
    I build and make things better where I can.
And if I fail it's not for lack of will
    But rather that I've raised too great a strife.

The days of man are three score years and ten,
    I hope there comes a time of quiet peace,
When battle's past and work is largely done
    And I can find retirement, then release.

*   *   *   *

Bury me near White Laggan bothy
    Where the orchids nod in the grass,
Where birds fly and furry hares run
    And men walk the mountain pass.

I have struggled and fought all my life long.
    Now shall I rest in peace
And lift mine eyes to the hills above,
    Or look down from God's house on high?

Many are called and given their task to do,
    To walk life's highways or tend a lone perfumed garden.
Many are called and may owe much to a few,
    But few are chosen.

*   *   *   *

I never moved to any sheltered bay,
    Running from challenges as they arose.
I never moved to any sheltered bay,
    When I have died let this be said of me.

Sur le Pont d'Avignon
(ou de Bailleul)

Au Collège de Bailleul,
    L'on y danse, l'on y danse,
Sur le pont de Bailleul,
    L'on y danse tout en rond.

Les beaux élèves font comme ceci.
    Les beaux maîtres font comme cela.
Sur le pont de Bailleul,
    L'on y danse tout en rond.

Dans le monde hors de Bailleul,
    L'on y danse, danse partout.
Danse au ciel, pont et chemin
    Menant je ne peux dire où.

Free Translation of the Above

Up at Oxford's Balliol College,
    The dance of life flows in full swing.
When not in the pursuit of knowledge
    Students and Dons "dance in a ring."

The bridge at Avignon is broken,
    Where lords and ladies used to meet.
The bridge of Balliol is but a token,
    A fantasy, saying "Life is Sweet."

In world at large the dance continues,
    Traffic reaching to the sky.
Where it tends (or will it finish?)
    No-one knows; at least not I.

Niagara Reflections

By the river of Niagara
Where the water rushes swiftly
In a curtain down the cliff face
I was seated meditating:

Why are we like cells in matter,
Jostling, pushing, rubbed together?
Moving as a flowing river
Down the cliff we seem to vanish.

Did all life once start by matter
Forming single cells in motion,
Did the single cells make contact
With each other, and increase life?

Once created, did life burgeon,
Slowly through the ages burgeon,
Gradually develop forwards,
Move on to its state at present.

It would seem so. Rushing water
Where the drops have flowed together
In a pattern of our lifetimes,
Showing certain variations.

But Niagara goes forward
On its own well-charted flight path.
Could there be a Plan eternal,
Aiding all the forward movement.

112

Titles

First Lines